FATHERLESS

REVEALING THE VOID AT HOME

By Amoo

Unless otherwise stated,
all Scripture quotations are taken from the
New King James Version of the Bible

FATHERLESS

ISBN : 978-9988-3-9603-9

TABLE OF CONTENTS

"And he will turn, the hearts of the fathers to the children, and the hearts of the children to their fathers, lest I come and strike the earth with a curse."

Malachi 4: 6

DEDICATION

Dedicated to my son,
and the many sons in spiritual development.

TESTIMONIALS

What Amoo has done in this magnificent work is to help us understand what the prophet Joel said in "Joel 2:28 KJV
– Bro. Nacoe Brown

"*This book is an excellent read. Our male generation is undoubtedly facing a crisis, and Amoo's insight into 'men being quietly assassinated' is prophetic. It is much needed by men of all ages, and I thank God for this anointed and timely release.*"
- Pastor Jeffrey T. Scott, Pastor, Singer

Songwriter, Unity Christian Ministries, Cleveland TN

"*This exceptional book has helped me to become a better son, brother, man, husband, and father. But most important, I have become a better servant for God.*"
– Richard Willis, Sankofa International Inc

FOREWORD

"And the son said unto him, Father, I have sinned against heaven, and in thy sight, and am no more worthy to be called thy son." (Luke 15:21)

The Lord Jesus told us about a profound parable with many eternal truths in the Parable of the Prodigal Son.

Fatherlessness can have a profound impact on a child's life, affecting their emotional, social, and psychological development, among others. Amoo carefully explains with scriptural and first-hand events this lethal phenomenon with the aim of jolting the reader to correct this anomaly.

Children can have emotional struggles: Feeling abandoned, low self- esteem: Difficulty developing a positive self-image, aggression, or substance abuse, trouble forming healthy relationships or attachments, identity issues: Struggling to define masculinity or femininity.

It's essential to note that every child's experience with fatherlessness is unique, and the severity of these effects can vary depending on individual circumstances.

Some children may experience few negative effects, while others may face significant challenges. If you or someone you know is affected by fatherlessness, consider seeking support through this masterpiece.

Allow the Holy Spirit to use this book to minister healing to you. Remember, healing and growth are possible with the right support and resources.

By William Aggrey-Mensah

A son of Bishop Dag Heward-Mills

PART I

THE ATTACK ON THE FATHER'S ROLE THAT LEAVES THE SONS VULNERABLE

Chapter 1

ASSASSINATION ATTEMPT

"The enemy of society is confusing gender, family, and a hope for a life of stability. Its primary weapon is our fathers".

- Abraham Lincoln

On a warm, dry day in Africa's Harmattan season, my father was sitting on the porch of our home, quietly observing the garden. I was eight years old, deeply fascinated by exploration. One of my adventures was to climb the mango tree in our garden, which my father could see perfectly from where he sat on the porch. With mangoes ripe for picking, I decided to climb the tree, shake down the fruits, and indulge in a delightful feast. The limitation I faced was my height; I wasn't tall enough to reach the closest branch of the mango tree. Positioned near the house's wall, the tree stood about nine feet tall and was protected by broken glass bottles on top of the wall. To overcome this, I placed a wooden chair under the tree for support. Despite my father's attentive watch from his seat, he remained silent as I ascended the tree. Stepping onto the chair, I stretched for the nearest branch, pulled myself up, and began shaking the tree energetically by jumping on its strongest branch. This action resulted in several ripe mangoes falling to the ground.

The floor under the mango tree in the garden was littered with the delightful dropping of ripe mangoes. My next step was to climb down from the tree, gather my treasure of mangoes, and then run to a hideout where I could indulge until I was full. I remember the mere thought alone of biting into those mangoes filled me with joy and excitement.

As I descended the lowest branch near the wall, I reached out for the chair, but my feet fell a few inches short of reaching it. Hanging from the branch, I stretched my toes toward the chair while my left hand hovered over the wall with the broken bottles. Eventually, I decided to let go and drop a two--inch fall onto the chair. Immediately I released my grip on the branch, and the chair collapsed beneath me. A searing pain shot through my left arm as the glass on the wall sliced through my flesh, making it bleed. Clutching my arm to stop the bleeding, I turned to my father, hoping for a comforting gesture, but he sat there motionless, his eyes distant and unresponsive. His lack of reaction left me feeling completely alone and abandoned.

With my mother and sisters away, I had no one to turn to for help. Even with my efforts to find a plant to stop the bleeding, the cut was too large for a leaf to cover. I resorted to using dirty rags to absorb the blood. Though the bleeding finally subsided, the pain was still excruciating. Upon my return, I set about cleaning up the blood, the fallen mangoes, and the shattered bottles and chairs. As I cleaned up the mess, supporting my injured arm, I couldn't help but watch my father's stillness on the porch, unmoved by the events unfolding before him.

Several months later, my mother noticed the scar and scolded me for not showing it to her sooner. While she acknowledged the physical scar, she remained unaware of the emotional impact of my father's coldness.

EMOTIONALLY ABSENT

The story of my father's emotional detachment is only a single instance of his absence throughout my upbringing. Regrettably, this account serves as only a small fraction of the more extensive issue that plagues our society--absent fathers in their sons' lives. This lack of emotional connection echoes with the attempt to eradicate paternal figures from our community.

"An emotionally absent father is like a shadow that lingers, a presence never truly felt, leaving behind a legacy of unanswered questions and unexpressed emotions."

FORMS OF ABSENCE

The role of a father is necessary in raising a son, but his absence can manifest in various ways: Physically, emotionally, spiritually, and even mentally.

It's unfortunate that despite the pivotal role of fathers, many households today don't have a physical father figure around. This affects young boys, leaving them feeling confused and lost. It's important to address this issue because it directly impacts the next generation of men who need guidance and support to succeed.

Dr. Michael Gurian, a family therapist and author of "The Wonder of Boys" in his book reiterates that boys develop their identity and character through watching 'Daddy' demonstrate strength, resilience and emotional intelligence. It is no wonder an average young man today does not possess the manliness of the men of old: Abraham, Isaac, Jacob and Mansa Musa and the likes who led their families, fed them, catered for both physical and spiritual needs and even left them huge inheritances. Ironically, women day by day are rising to fill the vacant shoes of fathers, the very person the world was created for to lead. The scripture below shows how God placed man in this important role.

Spiritual Principle: "And the LORD God took the man and put him into the garden of Eden to dress it and to keep it."

Genesis 2:15

In some homes, fathers are physically there but emotionally distant. They are cheerful and exciting everywhere except "Home." I've personally experienced how this emotional disconnection and guidance from a father figure can really hurt a young man's confidence leading to confusion and mistakes.

Many years ago, when it was time for Isaac to find a wife, he had a long chatty conversation with his father with the "specification" he needed in a wife. I'm sure he went on and on about the woman of his dreams being voluptuous, a proportionally accentuated body and of course a full lip and a sun-kissed skin. Abraham had a good laugh because Isaac was indeed looking for the wrong things in a woman. He sent his eldest servant to his relatives in Mesopotamia to find a wife for Isaac. And that's how Isaac was delivered from strange women to marry a virtuous woman, Rebekah.

Abraham knew what marrying a good woman could do for a man. Because of his wife Sarah's obedience to follow him wherever God led him, he became the wealthiest man ever to live. His relationship with his son Isaac sustained his wealth which has resulted in a prosperous generation.

A father's absence can go beyond just physical or emotional distance to spiritual detachment. This happens because many fathers don't have the knowledge or understanding of divine principles and universal laws required for effective parenting, which also serves as a protective covering over their sons. The inability of fathers to invest in such values often results in sons being unable to make positive contributions to society. Mental illness or dysfunction stemming from anxiety, depression, external pressure to provide for the family and stress can also prevent fathers from being there for their children, leaving their sons vulnerable to the negative influences of the world. David

Blankenhorn, in the book "Fatherless America: Confronting Our Most Urgent Social Problem", writes that "Fatherlessness is a gaping wound in the heart of our society, leaving countless children vulnerable and adrift."

Understanding these challenges can help us address them better, in order to break the generational curse of paternal ignorance and giving our sons the guidance they need to succeed.

"An absent father is like a ship that sails away, leaving behind a child stranded on the shore of longing and loss."

THE MYSTERY OF LIFE

Darkness surrounds our world every single day. The mere fact that we are blessed with a new day to experience life is a constant battle. Unfortunately, many individuals take this precious gift for granted and fail to understand the fullness of existence and the challenges that accompany it.

Young people, especially our sons, and often adults as well, take life for granted. Our society, ironically, is made up of life amid-darkness. Things like purpose, family, faith, and growth are the very essence of life in our time. On the opposite end of the spectrum is death, or darkness. Darkness, by definition, is non-existence, a beginning, or the absence of life, and it fights with life every day. When we embrace and understand this process of death and life in our lives, it eliminates the confusion that we deal with when we encounter struggles or face death situations. Things must first die to experience life.

"Death is not a defeat, but a gateway to a new adventure, where life takes on new meaning and purpose."This section will focus on expounding certain stages of life which include the germination process, fertilization, and a concept called casualties of war. This will help us understand some of the spiritual underlying factors of fatherlessness.

GERMINATION PROCESS

Life emerging from death, or vice versa, is evident in the germination processes. When a corn seed is planted in the soil, there is a simultaneous process of life and death. These processes continuously conflict, each vying for dominance.

I remember in my childhood; I worked on a small backyard farm that my family had for planting corn. I recall planting some corn seeds in the soil and wondering for a few days why the seedlings did not sprout up from the earth. As I grew older, I eventually realized through experience that in the process of corn seed germination, life was constantly battling against death. This became clear to me as I observed the germination process of the corn.

When a seed is planted in the ground, for a few days, the seed is dormant, at least its outer shell is. However, its life exists in the core of the seed itself, which is inside the outer shell. The outer shell, representing death, and it conflicts with the inner core for dominance. Yet, over time, as the outer shell decays in the soil, it gives way to the inner core, where new life exists. This results in the emergence of a live seedling shoot, representing new life. This process is a vivid illustration of the constant battle between life and death. It is one of the natural processes of life and embracing it can alleviate many of our problems.

As a child, I always lamented about the existence of war in our world. This sorrow was so profound that whenever I encountered any degree of conflict, I reacted with great dismay. Nevertheless, as I matured, my understanding deepened, and while I still disapprove of war, I began to embrace the cycle of life and death. This realization allowed me to live a more focused life, and my childhood ideals matured to the point where I realized that the battle between life and death is a natural process.

"Like a seed must die before it sprouts into new life, so too must we embrace endings as the beginning of something new."

FERTILIZATION PROCESS

In the process of fertilization, where the sperm seeks to fertilize the egg, there is a concurrent process of death and life co-existing, and sometimes life is born out of this process.

Millions of potential life cells swim toward the egg, attempting to fertilize it. However, in the struggle for life to emerge from death, only one life form triumphs, and that is you. Sometimes, two or more life forms are successful in fertilizing the egg and surviving. In this process, thousands of other potential life forms perish, symbolizing that for a few to live and fertilize the egg, some must die. Just as in the fertilization process, these stages of life battling against death are evident in everyday life, even as closely as they manifest within us daily.

"The beauty of fertilization is a reminder of life's fleeting nature, as the fragile beginnings of new life are often met with unexpected endings."

CASUALTIES OF WAR

This process of life warring against death, as mild or unseen as it may seem, is truly a battle for life and death. It is a war that extends beyond the casual eye, even manifesting inside us in everyday life.

Who gets to choose which seed will live to grow? Or who gets to choose which sperm will give rise to life by fertilizing the egg? The simplicity of this life-and-death struggle in our lives is often neglected by the casual observer, unaware that in our lives and those of our loved ones, there is a constant battle that can lead us to become "casualties of war." Therefore, with this knowledge in mind, I must be mindful of which side of the battlefield I am on and why, to avoid becoming a casualty of war.

A casualty of war is someone who, during conflict, is defeated and suffers injuries that hinder their progress. At times, we become casualties of war because we find ourselves in situations that set us back, such as divorce, child abuse, fatherless homes, or prisons. These circumstances can prevent us from experiencing life to its fullest. The unfortunate aspect of these setbacks is that we often stumble into them without consciously or subconsciously understanding how or why we ended up there.

Just as the process of life and death illustrates, this natural process of conflict is evident in life, suggesting that life is akin to war. Therefore, if we aim to live without succumbing to the status of casualties of war, we must identify why we are engaged in war in the first place.

To understand why we are involved in this war, we must consider a spiritual story that sheds light on this truth: the story of the fall in the Bible. This narrative can help illuminate why we find ourselves in this ongoing struggle.

"Life and death are in a constant struggle, and every moment we live is a triumph over the looming shadow of mortality."

WHAT IS THE WAR OF LIFE ABOUT?

In Isaiah 14:12-15 and Jude 9, the account of an angel's fall began in Heaven. Lucifer, an angel anointed to worship God, desired to be like God. In response to Lucifer's rebellion, God cast him out of heaven into darkness along with one-third of the angels who also rebelled. Jude 6 further explains this, stating that Lucifer and the rebellious angels are "reserved in everlasting chains under 'darkness' for the judgment of the great day."

Now, this darkness into which Satan was cast is the universe before its creation; it is darkness in its state of formlessness and void (Genesis 1:2). However, this darkness is not limited to the world, but it extends to the darkness in outer space, stretches to the realms of darkness beneath the sea, and into the deep recesses of darkness in men's hearts. After being cast down into darkness, Lucifer and the fallen angels now dwell on earth in all dark places, seeking to war against God and His glory, in life and its light.

Nonetheless, it is through the darkness on earth that God decided to show that His glory could be manifested in a fallen earth. To demonstrate this, God created man in contradiction, being both Earth-made from the soil and God-created from His breath (Genesis 2:7).

God placed humanity on a fallen earth (darkness), to lead lives of godliness (light), and to thereby glorify God in the midst of darkness. It is in the existence of our lives on earth that we have the lasting battle of life and death, good versus evil, highlighting God's glory against a fallen darkness that is evident in life.

To simplify the understanding of why we are at war, I will use the terms supernatural and natural. Supernatural refers to attributes or existence that relate to God and His domain, while natural pertains to existence or attributes that refer to Satan and the fallen world. The forces of darkness seek to prevent God's glory from being manifested on earth by attempting to destroy mankind. Therefore, the forces representing darkness—Satan, the demon angels, and the fallen world—are always seeking to destroy all that represents God, which is life and light.

This endless battle between life and death isn't just something external—it's also happening within us. Every day, as we go about our lives in these earthly bodies, our flesh and spirit are locked in a struggle. Understanding that this is a natural part of life helps us approach our lives more thoughtfully and avoid becoming casualties of this internal war.

Many of our great men and civil rights leaders in history experienced this reality, consciously or subconsciously becoming casualties of war. Figures such as Abraham Lincoln, Martin Luther King, Patrice Lumumba, Mahatma Gandhi, and

John F. Kennedy, who sought to lead their people out of darkness, faced this internal conflict between spirit and flesh in their souls.

"The conflict between the spirit and the flesh is a timeless struggle, a war waged within the depths of our souls."

AGAINST WHOM IS THIS WAR TARGETED?

There is an assassination occurring in our families, communities, and societies today that drastically affects us. Life is slowly being eradicated by the snares of darkness. The alarming aspect of this ongoing attempt is the silence in which it takes place.

Society consists of two foundational elements: a father and a mother. Out of these two, the father bears the seed of life while mothers nurture and deliver that life. However, the ongoing war has attempted to remove the father from this role by keeping the father out of life. Therefore, the father, as the bearer of life on earth, has been in the scopes of death since creation.

Collins Webster's Dictionary defines an Assassin as one who kills, especially a prominent person. In the context of this book, the reference to the assassination attempt refers to darkness being the assassin seeking to assassinate our fathers and young men.

In addition to being the seed of life on earth, the father is also a 'deliverer'. He is a deliverer in the sense that he ideally possesses great wisdom, knowledge, and understanding of life, especially concerning the snares of darkness. Therefore, at the very least, he is called to lead his home, guiding those under his headship away from the pitfalls of death, a lack of purpose in life, and deceptive darkness.

He is thus a 'deliverer' to those who are subject to the onslaught of the warring forces of darkness. The examples of our civil rights leaders and fathers in general speak to this deliverer role, especially those everyday fathers and home leaders who deliver others from the snares of darkness in this journey called life. In our society today, our species of fathers are becoming extinct due to this lasting battle against the forces that seek to eradicate life from our planet. Even the scriptures tell us about these forces we battle with.

Spiritual Principle: **"For we do not wrestle against flesh and blood, but against principalities, against powers, against the rulers of the 'darkness' of this age, against spiritual hosts of wickedness in the heavenly places."** (Ephesians 6:12, NKJV)

THE SERPENT'S CURSE

In the Bible, after the fall of man through Adam and Eve (Genesis 3), the serpent was cursed for deceiving Eve to disobey God. God cursed the serpent's seed to bear hatred against the woman's seed (Genesis 3:15). God stated that Eve's child would crush the head of the serpent and that the serpent would bruise the heel of her child.

This biblical pattern of hatred and war between the seed of the woman and the seed of the serpent holds the spiritual origin of the assassination attempt. This is because the references to Eve's child in the text foreshadow Christ, representing mankind, while the reference to the serpent's seed symbolizes Satan's kingdom of darkness and its fallen world. All over our world, there is an assigned strategy from the kingdom of darkness to destroy the child who will someday grow up to be a father and a bearer of the seed of life on earth.

"Demolishing what gives life is to defy the natural order of the universe."

11

ASSASSINATION ATTEMPT

The father is a representative of God's presence of life on earth, and this aggression on the father aims to sabotage the very essence of life through the death of this 'fatherhood' role in society. This attack takes different forms of eradication, ranging from spiritual to physical death and beyond.

This assassination attempt is a strategic attack that often goes unseen. In an effort to destroy the seed of life, this attack is evident in disease, addiction, broken homes, the unseen darkness of abusive fathers, and many other unseen causes that undermine the office of fatherhood.

Often, this darkness is hidden in generational curses in families, emotional death, and, most frequently, promiscuity in many homes. One of the most dangerous strategies in the assassination attempt against the seed of life is the early assassination or removal of the father or the 'man-child' from the home.

The number one strategy of death or darkness against fathers is to kill or destroy the seed of life when they are young. This explains why in many of our homes, fathers are removed from the lives of their sons at an early age, leaving them helpless to the onslaught of the assassination attempt.

This strategy of Satan aims to ensure that young boys are filled with fear from an early age leaving them timid, unguided, and lost in this world. This causes young men to become endangered species who cannot grow up to become fathers who can deliver themselves and many more families whom they lead. This is what Satan wants – to get rid of the father figures in the world to spread his kingdom of darkness.

The deliberate attempt to eliminate the father figure from their sons is a grave mistake that undermines the very foundation of family and society."

EARLY ATTEMPT

The Bible refers to two great fathers, Moses and Jesus, who were deliverers of many men. There is a clear example of the assassination attempt in the lives and stories of Moses and Jesus, which depicts the dangerous strategy of attacking our men early in their formative years. Interestingly, this pattern is greatly evident in our societies today.

In Moses and Jesus, we see the qualities of great deliverers of their people who were predestined to save many from death. Their lives were meant to be a catalyst for delivering people from death into life. This disbanded the forces of darkness, which oppose and destroy life. This early attempt against their lives follows a pattern aimed at assassinating young men in our society.

Moses was born into a Hebrew family and was destined to be a great deliverer of his people from Egyptian slavery. At the age of two, a decree was issued by the Pharaoh in Egypt to assassinate all two- year-old boys in the region.

I believe it was Moses' mothers' understanding of her child's identity and her awareness of the struggle between life and death that led her to take drastic measures to save him. She placed Moses in a reed boat and set him adrift in the river to protect him from the assassination attempt, which was a deadly assault. Similarly, before his birth in Bethlehem, Jesus was prophesied to be the "king of all kings," destined to liberate many people and deliver them from death into life.

As a deliverer in his own right, he also faced the same early assassination attempt as a child. The Bible tells us that when Jesus was two years old, King Herod issued a decree to kill all the two-year-old boys in the regions where Jesus was born. While his birth posed a threat to earthly kings, it was more significantly a threat to the forces of darkness because he was a source of life and deliverance for his people. Nevertheless, by divine intervention, he was spared through a message from an angel to his parents in a dream of the night, guiding them on how to escape the snares of darkness.

I believe that Jesus's parents understood his identity and were aware of the assassination attempt. If we aim to protect our sons from such threats, we must also be vigilant about potential attacks on their lives. It's critical to recognize the pattern of early assaults in our homes so that we can effectively combat this phenomenon.

"Warfare always surrounds the birth of a miracle "

WHAT ABOUT YOU?

Have you found yourself, at a young age, a victim of an assassination attempt? Or was your father removed from your home due to the many circumstances of life? Could it also be that you are a victim of this early attempt, and you are unconsciously living through a direct attack against your potential as a deliverer?

Many have found themselves asking these questions or hearing them spoken of in their communities by victims of this 'early attempt' against the seed of life. Questions such as why did my father die at a young age? How come my father never gets involved with me emotionally or spiritually? Why is my father not living in our home with me? Where did all the real men go? Why can't I find a good man to train my children? How come my father was never able to be a success? Why don't I know how to be a father myself? How come I did the same thing my father did in abandoning me? So many questions begging many answers...

Chapter 2

A FATHER'S ABSENCE

"The abandonment of a child leaves a burden they know not how to carry."

~ Thomas Edison ix

Thomas Edison's words echo so much truth even until today. The role of fatherhood has, and is under direct attack, so much so that it is important that we look at how these forms of attacks on fathers exist.

FORMS OF ASSASSINATION

In this direct attack against the seed of life and deliverer, there are many attempts in life, which are trying to assassinate the role of fatherhood. The fatherless epidemic is plagued by several forms of assassination. One of which is the lack of fathers having a personal and spiritual relationship with God.

Another form of this attempt to attack fatherhood is the lack of a father knowing his purpose as this often manifests itself through the absence of a father to teach his son. For if there is no father to teach a son, the son is left to the woes and the snares of darkness in society. The word of God speaks to a son listening to the advice of a father.

Spiritual Principle: "My son, forget not my law; but let thine heart keep my commandments: for length of days, and long life and peace shall they add to thee."

Proverbs 3:1-2 (NKJV)

Also, the snare of promiscuity can also be a form that attacks fatherhood. This promiscuity leads to broken homes that usually do not have the presence of the father to protect them from the snares of darkness in life.

Another factor is the mis-education of the position of fatherhood in our society and this leads to the assassination attempt against fatherhood.

Unfortunately, the absence of the father in society is one of the major reasons why our society is in its constant state of degradation. Our society has been left to the onslaught of these forces of darkness, which seek to destroy life by sabotaging the father. This absence leads to spiritual death in many forms, due to our society not having the covering of headships in our homes. A spiritual decay is creeping into our homes and societies, and this is becoming apparent through the violence in our streets, the promotion of promiscuity around our children, and the growing chaos in our society.

I argue that the erosion of respect for law and authority is a direct result of the ongoing assault on fatherhood. Our society is besieged by a deliberate drive against fathers and the premature loss of our sons, a threat that may already be at our doorstep. Today, we witness many of our son's falling victim to this assault, evident in the news, broken homes, communities, and overcrowded prisons. The violence and turmoil in our neighbourhoods can be traced back to our sons being left vulnerable to the perils of darkness. This vulnerability is an outcome of a systematic effort to strip them of their fathers' protection, rendering them prey to the absence of paternal authority. Without strong fatherly guidance, our sons are left exposed to the allure of a dark and dangerous world.

"A Father's absence is a major contributing factor to poverty, teenage pregnancy, juvenile delinquency, substance abuse, and other troubling social issues."

- National Center for Fathering

A FATHER IS A SYMBOL OF AUTHORITY

The principle of authority is pervasive in all aspects of society. To function effectively, one must learn to be submissive to authority and understand how to operate within it.

Authority is embodied in fatherhood, ideally serving as a son's first introduction to the principle of authority in the world. Therefore, how a son conducts this initial encounter with authority at home often becomes his reference point for the future. Our interactions within our homes, workplaces, churches, and the broader structure of societal governance can be viewed through the lens of our early relationship with our father figure. From this perspective, a principle emerges: those who succeed in society often excel in their dealings with authority.

Ideally, a father serves as the first authority figure in a young boy's life. However, if this initial impression of authority is marred by the father's absence, it can negatively impact the boy's understanding of authority figures in the future. Unless there are interventions by coaches, teachers, or mentors to provide a positive example of authority, the son may struggle. Without a positive understanding of authority, the son may face challenges in steering life and interacting with other authorities in society.

"Respect for authority is the mark of a mature person, and one of the hallmarks of a civilized society."

A FATHER IS A SCHOOL OF TRAINING

The presence of a fatherly figure serves as both the training ground for manhood and the foundation for a son's success in life. This is why the absence of a father is a significant detriment to the upbringing of our sons in society.

A father must be able to command the obedience of his son to create the necessary environment for training. In this setting, the father can teach the son essential principles applicable to mature interactions in society. As the first authority figure, the father sets the standard for how other authorities will be perceived by the son. Therefore, the absence of this positive authority figure creates a false impression of all authority the son will encounter in life. This misunderstanding can lead the son to be angry at all authority figures in society.

The scripture below echoes a key principle for fathers that are vital to the success of our sons and our societal structure:

Spiritual Principle: **"And ye fathers provoke not your children to wrath: but bring them up in the nurture and admonition of the Lord." Ephesians 6:4 NKJV.**

For fathers, it is important to not provoke their children into anger. Anger is an intense emotion, especially when it is sustained over time. It is easy to develop a dislike for someone due to a circumstance or misunderstanding, but when this dislike is fuelled by repeated provocation, it can turn into anger. If this anger continues day after day, it becomes the kind of anger described in the scripture. When a son is consumed by this anger, he can be misled by his emotions and may even seek to distance himself from his father's guidance and the training he provides.

However, sons also have a responsibility to be obedient to their fathers and to avoid being provoked to anger. The scripture suggests that a son's obedience to his father is a condition for a long and successful life (Ephesians 6:1-3). Through obedience, a son puts himself in a position to receive the necessary training under authority for his life.

QUESTIONS TO CONSIDER:

- What if a son was born without a father?

- What if a son yearned for his father's nurturing and guidance, but his father was physically absent from the home?

- What if a father was physically present but emotionally disconnected from his son's needs?

- What if a father was physically present but lacked the knowledge or understanding of how to fulfil his role as a godly, spiritually grounded father?

THE IRONY OF A GOODY-TWO-SHOES

Do you recall the high school boy everyone dubbed a goody-two-shoes? He was the one in oversized clothes, the scrawny kid who never caught the eye of the popular girls, the one who never ventured where the popular kids did.

Perhaps you don't remember him because you were that person. If so, congratulations! Goody-two-shoe types weren't seen as cool back then, at least not by the standards of the popular kids. They often faced teasing for not following the crowd.

I'm here to champion the goody-two-shoes! Many of them, as we grew up, became successful and purposeful because they stayed away from harm long enough to achieve success.

Even those who lacked a father's guidance benefited from their obedience, which kept them under the authority's training long enough to receive blessings. This obedience and submission, seen in the "goody-two-shoes syndrome," are key reasons for their success in society.

Whether this obedience is demonstrated directly or indirectly, it drives these young men towards future success and purpose in life. The irony of the goody-two-shoes syndrome lies in the blessings of success and purpose that stem from their obedience under the father's covering. In contrast, our uncovered sons, who have grown disobedient, face a potential curse due to the father's absence.

"To be obedient to the father is to be obedient to the future."

OUR UNCOVERED SONS

When a son grows up without the guidance of their fathers are left uncovered. The absence of a father causes our sons to seek their identity outside of themselves. What does this mean? According to the principle of the master and disciple, a son who has a father's guidance ideally surpasses their father in success. However, in the father's absence, a son without this guidance often seeks their identity in things other than themselves. This search outside of their father can lead to pride, anger, envy, and competition, which can hinder a son's success.

When the father figure is absent from the home, our sons may gravitate toward negative influences that misdirect them. These negative influences fill the void left by fatherlessness with self-destructive lifestyles that hinder the pursuit of long life and success. This truth underscores the fact that the absence of fatherhood will always be filled by some form of influence if left unchecked.

"Nature abhors a vacuum."

A FALSE IDENTITY

While seeking their identity outside of themselves, our sons develop low self-esteem, leading them to create a false identity. This false identity is often given to them by negative influences that fill the void left by an absentee father. In many cases, this void is filled by peer pressure groups that can evolve into scandalous gangs.

This process of seeking their identity externally can lead our sons to adopt false names that match their false identity. They abandon the real names given to them by their fathers and adopt street names to mask the pain of their absent fathers. These street names often usher them into fulfilling the stereotype associated with the chosen name, such as "Slick," which implies becoming a deceptive thief, womanizer, or alcoholic. The name itself symbolizes deception.

"If you don't know who you are, the world will tell you who you're not"

A STORY OF ABSENCE

My friend once told me a story about a twelve-year-old boy from a well-to- do family in Georgia, and how he coped with the absence of his father and the lack of parental guidance.

One day, he and his friends were at our home talking, and the conversation turned to things they disliked. As they took turns, this boy blurted out that he hated his parents. When asked why, he said that all they did was argue and that they never spent any time with him. While discussing this sensitive issue, his anger escalated, and he told his friends that he was planning to harm his parents because he felt neglected by them. It was evident that this young son was being provoked to anger day after day.

When I heard this story, I was shocked. To me, it highlighted the extent of the emotional absence of a father's guidance over his son. What really alarmed me was that this twelve-year-old boy had reached a point of entertaining such thoughts, yet it seemed his anger had gone unnoticed at home. I feared that one day; the wrong influence would reach him and lead to an unthinkable outcome.

Chapter 3

GENERATIONS CURSED

"Damn the man who I would have called father, I blame him for who I am"

~Charles Manson

I
f you knew who Charles Manson became, you would understand the accuracy of his quote regarding the absence of fathers and how it can become a curse to a son. Indeed, the office of fatherhood is temporary in this life. This office is ordained by God and is designed to provide the direction and training necessary to nurture a young man aspiring to enter the office of fatherhood. This office of fatherhood is ordained by God to protect and guide a family under the leadership of the father so that families can receive all the blessings that God has for them in this life.

This office ordained by God has implications in the full understanding of God's system: a system of order and structure through the father that resembles the system of God's heavenly order and structure. This system of God shows that God is sovereign over all things, that He is the creator of heaven and earth, that Christ is the son of God, and that the angels, who are below Christ, represent God's workmen.

In God's kingdom, the order and structures are clearly defined: God as the head, Christ as the intermediary, and the angels as the workmen. This heavenly order can be likened to the structure of the home, with the father, the mother, and the children. This parallel between the divine and family structures suggests that God represents the father, Christ represents the mother, and the angels represent the children.

As my mentor often said, "God thinks it, Christ speaks it, and the angels do it." Similarly, in the family, we can see the father formulating instructions, the mother conveying them, and the children carrying them out. This parallel ordained by God provides insight into how order and structure function within authority.

This family structure, representing a godly presence on earth, is important for society's welfare. It serves as the ordained training ground by God to prepare a son for success in society. When the father operates according to godly principles within the home structure, he invites the blessings of God's kingdom into his home. This explains why, when a son grows up with an absent father and develops a misunderstanding of fatherhood and authority in general, it can be challenging for him to believe in and have a relationship with God. His perception of authority has been tainted from the beginning by his father's absence.

GOD THE AUTHOR

When we contemplate the attributes of God, such as His sovereignty, Him being the Highest, a provider, defender, counsellor, and the Almighty, one of the most crucial attributes we discover is that God is the maker of heaven and earth, the creator of all things. This makes God the creator and author of all things, including human life. The word "authority" is derived from "author," **implying** that if God is the maker and author, then He has control or authority over all that He makes. I have never encountered anyone who creates something and is not the master of his creation. An author will always possess all authority over their creation.

This similarity of authorship holds true in the case of the father and the son. Since the father is the bearer of the seed of life on earth and the maker of a son, he is designed to have authority over all that he creates. He is, therefore, by default, God's chosen authority over creation on earth. Due to the absence of fathers in many homes and the strategic attack on the teaching of knowledge through fatherhood, there is a great misunderstanding around the importance that the father plays as an authority in our homes and societies.

FATHERLESSNESS CAN EXPOSE YOU TO A REBELLIOUS SPIRIT

One reason our sons sometimes struggle in society is the lack of a father figure, which can lead them to develop a distorted view of authority and fatherhood. This lack of respect for fatherhood can instigate our sons to challenge fathers and other authorities.

Alongside the challenges faced by fatherless sons, our culture subtly promotes disrespect for authority. This disrespectful attitude fosters a rebellious spirit, causing our sons to be disobedient to authority. Unknown to them, by rebelling against earthly authority, they are indirectly rebelling against God, as He established these authorities. This rebellion can result in many curses for our sons.

Rebellion often begins in the heart and is reflected in words. Growing up without a father figure, a son may harbour anger and resentment, which can manifest in disrespectful words and behaviours towards authority figures.

UNCOVERING HIS NAKEDNESS

The story of Noah and his sons in the scriptures (Genesis chapter 6 to 9) provides insight into the attitude of a rebellious son. Noah, chosen by God to save His people from the flood, was also a leader and the father of three sons: Shem, Ham, and Japheth. After leading God's people to safety, Noah became drunk and was found naked outside his tent.

Ham, one of Noah's sons, dishonoured his father by speaking ill of his nakedness and exposing his drunkenness as a public spectacle. This act was a direct insult to the authority established by God. In contrast, Shem and Japheth, the other sons of Noah, covered their father's nakedness and showed respect by not looking at him as they brought him back into his tent.

Upon sobering up, Noah cursed Ham for his disrespectful behaviour and blessed Shem and Japheth. Despite Noah's mistake of being drunk in public in the first place, he still retained the authority to bless and curse as he was still operating in the office of fatherhood and a deliverer ordained by God. Therefore, Ham had no right to speak disrespectfully towards Noah, just as fatherless sons have no right to speak angrily against their absent fathers or any authority figure.

A CURSED GENERATION

Many sons growing up without fathers have found themselves burdened by a curse, as they've spoken ill of the fatherhood institution. This includes generations of sons who've misunderstood the concept of fatherhood and authority. This misconception starts as a seed of thought and grows into rebellious words, often resulting in chaotic actions within our communities. The scripture below describes this curse of chaos and destruction as a cruel messenger, which has become inherent in our society due to the rebellion festering within evil hearts.

Spiritual Principle: **An evil man seeks only rebellion; therefore, a cruel messenger will be sent against him." (NKJV, Proverbs 17:11)**

A CRUEL MESSENGER

What, then, is this cruel messenger? It is a common understanding that wherever rebellion dwells, so does an evil heart. The scriptures emphasize that where this evil heart of rebellion resides, a cruel messenger will be sent against it. This cruel messenger is evident in the generation of our sons who rebel against authority. An unmistakable sign of the presence of this cruel messenger is the evidence of disorder and destruction. It is not coincidental that wherever there is disorder and destruction, rebellion is present.

An evident example can be seen in the disorder and destruction caused by gangs in our decent neighbourhoods. This signifies that an increasing number of the youth bracket are rebelling against anything that represents order and structure in authority.

Moreover, there is another aspect of the curse of the cruel messenger, which manifests as destruction. When a son rejects the authority of his father in rebellion, a cruel messenger of destruction is sent against him. This destruction leads the son to act on his potential abilities without any guidance. This lack of guidance often drives them to engage in criminal activities, leading to the destruction of our sons and their communities. This is evident in the overcrowding of prisons and the self-inflicted destruction of our homes, which erodes the moral fabric of our communities.

The cruel messenger, who brings disorder and destruction, aims to eliminate the father and the sons, leaving the moral structure of our society vulnerable. After all, to defeat or destroy anything, one must first destroy the headship. In this case, the father is the stronghold in society. He is the head, the strongman, and his successors, the sons, are all targeted for destruction.

SINS OF THE FATHER

Another consequence of the cruel messenger is the perpetuation of generational curses, also known as the sins of the fathers, which are passed down through families.

These curses often manifest in various forms of vices such as alcoholism, long histories of imprisonment, and instances of molestation, abuse, and even suicide, spanning multiple generations and wreaking havoc on families. This cycle continues until one generation consciously chooses to break free from it. When a son is deprived of his father's covering, he also misses out on the opportunity to learn about these generational curses that have afflicted his family for so long.

This lack of awareness leaves him navigating life without a clear understanding of the challenges that have affected the men in his family for generations. Hence, he may unknowingly fall into the same destructive patterns that ensnared his ancestors.

Fact: Without the awareness of the curses afflicting your family, you might unknowingly perpetuate them in your own life.

This understanding of the curses can lead to immediate success, as it serves as a catalyst for making the right decisions and avoiding the same mistakes as our fathers.

Many of our sons who find themselves in prison are simply repeating the same destructive cycle as their fathers. Similarly, some families struggle to find success because they continue to face the same setbacks.

Imagine if a generation broke free from this cycle, keeping their sons out of prison and providing them with proper fatherly direction.

This would enable their sons to overcome the curse of imprisonment and surpass their fathers. Such a change would pave the way for success in future generations, as each successive generation would be free to pursue education and reach new heights of achievement.

PART II

HOW THE FATHERLESS ISSUE AFFECTS A SON

Chapter 4

WRESTLING WITH AUTHORITY

"Authority, to a child is the covering by which he operates. Without it, he is doomed to a life of struggle."

Charles Stanley

It was a quiet Monday at home. My mother was at work, and my sister had gone shopping with friends, leaving just my father and me in the house. The absence of the others created a stillness that settled over the home.

As an adolescent, I was in the midst of transitioning from boyhood to manhood. I began to experience the physical signs of maturity, such as increased muscular strength, which made me feel capable of defending myself against my siblings' bullying.

Standing by the swing door in the kitchen, my father entered and asked me to go to the corner store to buy him some shaving cream. I hesitated, feeling a sense of defiance towards him due to his lack of presence in my life. In a moment of anger, I raised my voice, refusing to go to the store for him. His response was firm; he insisted that I go, regardless of my feelings.

Fuelled by a false sense of youthful strength and rebellion, I felt emboldened to challenge him. However, my father quickly subdued me in a wrestling match, demonstrating his physical superiority. Pinned to the floor, I realized the futility of my rebellion and begged him to release me. He did so, admonishing me for my disrespect and disobedience.

Left alone on the kitchen steps, I reflected on the incident, realizing it was a manifestation of the inner turmoil I harboured towards my father's absence in my life.

This incident of anger that was fuelled by thoughts of my father's absence stirred a sense of pride that caused me to challenge my authority.

In Bishop Dag Heward-Mills' book series "Loyalty and Disloyalty", he reveals in his book "Those Who Are Dangerous Sons" that "When sons begin to have arguments with their fathers, they reveal how big and proud they have become, just like it shares in the scripture below.

Spiritual Principle: **"By pride comes nothing but strife... (NKJV, Proverbs 13:10 (a))**

CHALLENGING AUTHORITY

Many of our sons, who have experienced the absence of a father, often exhibit a challenging spirit during adolescence, particularly towards established authority figures. Through conversations with these rebellious sons, I've discovered that the root cause of their defiance is often deep-seated anger towards their fathers. This anger is sometimes so ingrained that sons may not consciously recognize it, evident in statements like, "I don't care about my father, he was not around anyway," or "I don't know that man, he was never there for me."

Despite their denial, their tone and body language betray the underlying anger towards their fathers. This anger catalyses their defiance against authority. Preferably, the father should be the first authority figure a son encounters, but if this encounter is marred by anger, it distorts the son's perception of authority in general.

DRY TEARS

As stated, the signs of a son's anger can sometimes go unnoticed unless observed by someone who understands the plight of a fatherless son. A son's resentment against authority often manifests as a phenomenon I call "dry tears."

There is a subculture among our sons that dictates young men should not show any signs of emotion or weakness through tears. Instead, they are encouraged to express their genuine emotions and pain through other forms, or what I refer to as "dry tears." This culture of suppressing tears causes our sons to bottle up their emotions and bury their anger deeply, leading to a hardened outlook on life. This is unfortunate because tears and emotions are meant to be the wellsprings of life that initiate the healing process from our pain.

These forms of "dry tears" manifest in drug addictions, envy, suicide, bullying, promiscuity, and seeking approval from peers; behaviours that society often views as rebellious acts. However, I submit to you that these actions by our sons are, in fact, a masked cry for help from society.

FALSE AUTHORITY

In the absence of a father's authority, our sons are drawn, in their adolescent vulnerability, towards peer groups that fill the void left by fatherhood. These peer pressure groups act as false authorities because, according to the order and structure of God reflected in the family, they have not been appointed as the headship over our sons.

When I speak of false authority, I am referring to the negative influences that fill the vacuum of an absent father. These peer pressure groups, seen as false authorities, exacerbate the phenomenon of "dry tears"; within these groups, it is taught that crying and showing emotion is unacceptable for a young man.

This drives our sons to seek the approval of these false authorities by engaging more in bullying or displaying toughness. These false authorities consist of rebellious youths who are often acting out due to misdirection and anger. They often form a nucleus resembling a family to compensate for the absence of fatherhood and the family structure. Lacking the nurturing experience, these false authorities often lead our sons towards a destructive life, including involvement in promiscuity, and other harmful behaviours.

PLIGHT OF PROMISCUITY

The impact of peer pressure in promoting a subcultural lifestyle of promiscuity is a significant destructive force affecting both our sons and daughters in society.

One common initiation rite in these groups is to demonstrate how many women a young man can sleep with, creating pressure for him to be promiscuous to gain peer approval. This pressure is detrimental to both the individual and society. What makes this plight even more tragic is that it has little to do with the young women involved or the approval sought from these groups.

In the absence of a father figure, young girls sometimes seek solace in the callous attention of a superficial young man. However, the deeper issue lies in the son's search for paternal approval. Because he did not receive this approval, he goes to great lengths, including engaging in promiscuity, to seek it from his peers.

This should prompt a reader to ask similar questions in their community about the pattern of promiscuity in our sons, which is often motivated by the absence of their fathers.

ESAU'S PLIGHT

In Genesis chapter 25 verses 29 to 35, the Bible tells a story about two brothers: Esau and Jacob. Esau was the oldest son of Isaac, while Jacob was the younger son. Due to his desire for instant gratification, Esau sold his birth right to Jacob for a morsel of bread and lost his blessing as the firstborn. Before Isaac's death, he mistakenly blessed Jacob instead of Esau, leading to Esau feeling under-blessed, which felt like a curse to him. This caused Esau to develop hatred towards his brother Jacob, who received the father's blessing by mistake. Esau's resentment highlights a spirit of challenging authority that arises when a son is not under the father's blessing.

Esau's anger not only led him to consider killing his brother but also to act in defiance of his father's wishes by taking a wife from the daughters of Canaan. When Isaac instructed Jacob not to take a wife from the Canaanites, Jacob obeyed. However, Esau, displeased with his father's directive, married Mahalath, the daughter of Ishmael, in addition to his many wives.

WRITTEN OFF

Many adults perceive instances of promiscuity in our sons as acting out. However, the truth is that when a son starts acting out, it indicates that he is wrestling with authority in his heart. This internal struggle often goes unnoticed by casual observers, as it primarily occurs within the son's heart and mind. This struggle signifies that the son is beginning to resent authority, feeling that authority figures should have been present to teach him how to be a man.

Misunderstanding our sons' cries for help often leads them to be dismissed by their fathers, mothers, and society at large. Being dismissed in this way causes them to seek a sense of belonging from false authorities or peer pressure groups. Within these groups, they learn subcultures that promote a disregard for the law. This deepens their misunderstanding of authority, leading to lawlessness and legal troubles.

Chapter 5

MOTHER'S FAVOURITE

"I can't love him any more than I do, and monetary gestures are temporary. What I would give to be able to fill the space that belongs to his father."

~Tami Nanetta Ralston

In our current generation, the role of a mother has become more prominent in the raising and upbringing of sons. This increased role has made mothers the backbone of our community in the absence of fathers. Assuming both parenting roles has often made mothers the favoured parent of sons.

This favouritism is frequently apparent when sons achieve success. They often express gratitude to their mothers immediately after thanking God for being the reason for their success in life. Sometimes, sons thank only their mothers, without mentioning God, indicating the level of importance the mother holds in the son's life.

Many successful men, especially in sports, frequently express their gratitude first to God and then to their mothers when they achieve success. Each time this happens, it points up the gap between the presence of mothers and the absence of fathers in the lives of our sons. In the father's absence, the mother becomes the favourite due to the significant role she plays in the upbringing of sons. To the son, the mother becomes the primary figure who is present to empathize with his struggles as he matures into a man.

Due to the father's absence in the home, many mothers have to now work two jobs to fulfill the daunting role of the sole provider and carer. Further, she makes herself emotionally available by being a loving, nurturing mother who tutors her son to become a respectable man in his community. Through her example, she also becomes a model for the kind of woman her son might choose as a future wife.

In fulfilling these roles, the mother ensures her son is healthy and well-provided. While juggling these responsibilities, she also attempts to fill the void of fatherhood, imagining how a father would raise his son in his absence. This dual parenting role is one of the most profound acts of servitude that mothers undertake.

In today's generation, the act of single mothers raising their sons alone is one of the most self-sacrificial acts. While dying for someone is the ultimate sacrifice, mothers demonstrate their sacrifice in numerous ways by putting aside their own needs and dedicating their lives to their fatherless sons.

A LIONESS

The strength of mothers in their daily sacrifices can be likened to the sacrificial nature of a lioness, which bravely balances life's dangers while providing and protecting her young. When I reflect on my mother and how she raised me amidst unseen obstacles, her courage against all odds reminds me of the strength and spirit of a lioness.

This image of bravery is prominent in the animal kingdom, particularly in lions, where the female, or lioness, raises her cubs, hunts for food, and nurtures them in the wild, protecting them from various dangers. While the lioness does all the work, the male lion appears relaxed, lounging in the shade, and grooming himself. Despite his seemingly lazy demeanour, the male lion is at least present in the animal family, serving as a model of fatherhood to the lioness's cubs.

In contrast, it's a sombre reflection that even in the animal kingdom, which lacks human-like reasoning abilities; these creatures seem to understand the importance of family structure better than we do as humans. Perhaps our human ability to reason has led us to overcomplicate things, moving us away from the simple yet profound order and structure evident in God's creation, particularly in families.

IRREPLACEABLE ROLE

Even though mothers in our generation are striving and achieve results in their dual parenting role, the role of fathers is irreplaceable in raising a son, particularly in balancing the gender dynamics of our societal structure.

When a son enters the trial-and-error phase of manhood, a mother may feel defeated because she cannot speak the language of a father. This is when mothers often try to introduce coaches and mentors to fill the void of fatherhood temporarily. While these replacements can help mitigate the absence of fathers, they can never fully replace the authenticity of a biological father who operates according to godly principles in the home.

You may have heard the saying, "It takes a man to raise a man." This wise saying holds true, especially during a son's formative adolescent years. As a son matures and discovers his identity as a man, he needs a father figure to guide him through this stage. Before this stage, a mother's nurturing is sufficient, balancing the absence of a father, but this over-nurturing may have its downsides.

MOTHER'S WORDS

There are certain challenges and shortcomings in the dual parenting role of mothers, particularly in raising sons. Some mothers, frustrated by the absence of their sons' fathers, may express their frustrations through harsh words directed at their sons. Even as a son of a single mother, it is difficult for me to fully grasp the depth of these frustrations. However, I can imagine that seeing similarities between a son and his absent father could serve as a painful reminder of the father's absence, often triggering emotions related to a failed relationship or marriage, or to grave sacrifices that go untold.

Some mothers who are left to be the sole caretakers of their sons due to the father's absence may develop resentment towards the father. This resentment can manifest indirectly through words directed at the son, such as, "You're going to be just like your trifling daddy," or "You remind me of your deadbeat daddy." These words can have a profound impact on a son's psyche, potentially leading to rebellion. Since a son often resembles his father, these words are indirectly aimed at the father but affecting the son, it can significantly influence a son's development for better or for worse.

I encourage mothers, regardless of their circumstances, to choose their words carefully, as their words can either build their son's masculine esteem or scar his identity and trigger resentment towards his father and other authority figures. These words are the foundation upon which a son builds his identity, especially in the absence of his father.

Therefore, mothers must use positive reinforcement in their language such as:

- Keep your son aware of his father's love even when he's not present.

- Express your pride in him as he grows into a young man.

- Support his endeavours, even if they don't personally interest you.

- Avoid telling him he reflects his father's negative traits.

These words of encouragement serve as a temporary shield in the absence of a father. Since the mother is the sole support for a fatherless son, her words act as a spiritual shield over him. A mother must adjust her tone when speaking to her son, as mothers are naturally motivators. If her nurturing instinct is genuine, then her spiritual nurturing through her words will have a profound impact, potentially shaping his life for better or for worse. The bible speaks about the power of mother's words below:

Spiritual Principle: **"Death and life are in the power of the tongue, and those who love it will eat its fruit." (NKJV, Proverbs 18:21)**

MOTHER'S FAVOURITE

In the absence of the father, the son often becomes the mother's favourite. Just as the mother is there for the son in his struggles, the son reciprocates by being available for the mother in her own challenges. Moreover, the mother has a God-given opportunity to shape her son into the kind of husband she desires. This underscores the importance of the mother choosing her words carefully with her fatherless son, as she can mould him into a great father and man. Many grateful daughters have been blessed with well-rounded men for marriage thanks to mothers who have raised their sons with care.

These sons are the result of a mother's sacrificial efforts in raising a man who can potentially break the cycle of fatherlessness in their family. In the absence of a father, the son becomes a partner to the mother and indirectly assumes the role of the man of the house, despite lacking any formal fatherly training. This unique relationship causes the son to receive some favouritism from the mother.

Fact: A mother's favouritism could lead her to overcompensate.

Playing the double, when it comes to parenting, often leads to a shortcoming: the mother's tendency to over-compensate towards her son, manifesting in various forms. At times, a mother may feel responsible for the absence of her son's father, prompting her to compensate by allowing the son to assume the father's role. This over-compensation can have a negative impact, subconsciously instilling a mind-set of foolish pride.

As an over-compensation tool, a mother may allow her son to be promiscuous with young girls, treating him as if he were an adult man. This over-compensation is dangerous and creates confusion about the mother-son relationship dynamics. This issue of over-compensation can have lasting effects on a son's future relationships with women, as he may become accustomed to getting whatever he wants due to his mother's actions

Not only does this over-compensation train the son to approach life thinking he can have anything he wants when he wants, but it can also lead to destructive outcomes. When reality shows him that he cannot have everything he desires, the son may develop a defeatist mentality, causing him to seek destructive alternatives. Although a mother strives to do her best in raising her fatherless son, there is no replacement that can fill the void of a father.

This role is ordained by God, and in the order and structure that God ordained for the balance of our society, fathers are irreplaceable. Our world requires the balance of a father being present in the life of a son. Even though mothers try to raise their sons into good men, there will always be a void in the hearts of sons who do not have a father. This void can only be filled by fathers and by the choices of sons to become the next generation of fathers to come.

Chapter 6

A SON'S CHOICE

Be careful to leave your sons well instructed rather than rich, for the choices of the instructed are better than wealth of the ignorant."

~Epictetus

Webster's Dictionary defines 'choice' as "The act or power of choosing; an alternative, [one of two choices]." While Collins Dictionary seeks to define the word, it sheds minimal light on the alternatives that a son has to choose from in a father's absence.

Individuals who make decisions bear personal responsibility for their choices, as we steer the ultimate vehicle of our bodies toward our destinies. Every right or wrong turn falls on our decisions. Every split second becomes a decision-making fraction that magnifies the everyday struggle of human beings in choosing to be good or bad, to succeed or fail, to be right or wrong.

The key to our choices lies in the resolve we muster when making up our minds. Some refer to this resolve as the actual act of deciding. Spiritually minded individuals might see this key as a force, like faith, that inspires us to take something that does not exist and bring it into existence.

Conversely, this resolve can be a fear that causes us to doubt our ability to succeed, leading to failure. This power of fear can cause people to give up when the going gets tough.

The alternatives of faith or fear, ingrained through external influences we digest, are separated by a choice that exists in our minds. These influences affect our choices and make choice the bridge that leads us to the gate of our destinies. I have come to find that this driving force in choice has two extremes: An extreme of a positive outcome - success, and an extreme of a negative outcome - failure.

SON'S CHOICE

In the case of a son with an absentee father, does his choice to become a success or failure rest solely on him? Does the decision to become a menace to society lie solely on the shoulders of a fatherless son? What about the son who strives and overcomes the obstacles of fatherlessness? Should he be solely recognized for his ability to overcome, or should he share the glory of his triumphs with others?

Removing the aspect of reward or blame, especially regarding the failure of fatherless sons in society, raises questions that have divided families and individuals, as it forces them to confront the possibility of bearing responsibility for failure. To some extent, I agree. However, I also disagree because even though a young man's decisions are his own, some of our sons do not have a choice in controlling the influences that come into their minds.

UNTOLD STORIES

You may have heard a rags-to-riches story about a son who was born fatherless and yet overcame those obstacles to become a success story from a fatherless home. These stories often make headlines and receive heartfelt attention because of the hope they inspire in overcoming life's challenges.

I appreciate these inspiring stories myself. However, when you are in the trenches with fatherless sons who have failed to overcome their circumstances, you immediately sense the disparity between success stories and the harsh reality. For every successful fatherless son, there are thousands of others whose stories of failure do not make the headlines.

Many of these sons who do not make the headlines turn out to be failures in society. Most of the time, their demise is brought about by their own choices—choices that lead them down paths of destruction in violence, waywardness, promiscuity, suicide, and the wickedness spreading in our world, originating from impoverished minds.

However, I have come to realize that a young son's mind is fragile and vulnerable to the impressions placed upon him, even though the decisions regarding success or failure ultimately lie with the son. These choices are influenced by the powers that captivate the youthful mind of a fatherless son.

WHAT'S IN HIS MIND

Many of these sons, who never make the headlines, end up as failures in society. Often, their downfall is a result of their own choices—choices that lead them down paths of violence, waywardness, promiscuity, suicide, and the kind of wickedness that originates from impoverished minds.

However, I've come to realize that a young son's mind is fragile and vulnerable to the impressions placed upon him, even though the decisions regarding success or failure ultimately lie with the son. These choices are influenced by the powers that captivate the youthful mind of a fatherless son.

Some of the factors that influence a son's choices are those that inundate his mind-set. Factors such as a son's peers play a crucial role in influencing him as he searches for an identity. These friends who shape a son's mind-set become critical to his choices, which is why sons easily swayed by their friends often find themselves in trouble.

The family also plays a role in shaping a son's mind-set. A family structure that teaches godly principles can develop a mind-set in a son that enables him to withstand negative influences and obstacles. When a father and mother are actively involved in a son's life, they become a defence against wrong influences that could lead a son towards a mind-set of failure.

Another factor that influences a son's mind-set is his ability to know his self-worth, which often comes from his father. This instils a confidence that shields him from adopting a negative mind-set under the influence of others. Confidence is a lesson that a father should impart to his son from a young age so that his self-assurance is built on the foundation of his youth.

A FATHER'S TRAINING

Finally, another significant factor influencing a son's mind-set is the emotional environment to which he is exposed. This external emotional influence can sway a son's choices towards either success or failure. Whether this environment is positive or negative, it plays a crucial role in shaping a son's mind-set.

Ideally, a son's father serves as the frontline defence in guarding his mind against the onslaught of negative influences that seek to corrupt it. This guardian role requires a father to educate his son about his identity before other negative forces can influence him.

If a father is the living, example of the godly principles he teaches his son, the son will have the power, through his father's example, to make positive choices. This power comes from the son's submission to the authority of his father. When a son submits to the teaching of godly principles from his father, his mind-set is trained to yield to authority.

Therefore, his choices will follow the path of righteousness in authority, due to the son's tendency to be submissive.

In the case of an absentee father, a subconscious negative emotion can be instilled because a son does not receive a sense of worth from a father's love. These influences from peers, family, godly principles, emotions, and self-knowledge can shape a son's mind and the choices he makes, leading to either a negative or positive outcome in his life. These influences become teaching grounds that establish a son's mind-set and his journey through life, echoing the truth of the principle below:

Spiritual Principle: **"Train up a child in the way he should go, and when he is old, he will not depart from it." (NKJV, Proverbs 22: 6)**

This spiritual principle dictates that whatever forces a son is exposed to; he is trained to become that. This training can come from emotions, a lack of self-knowledge, peers, parents, godly principles, or whatever influences are shaping our sons. Therefore, if he is learning in an environment that is training him to be a success, he will become a success. Conversely, if he is in an environment of failure, he will likely become a failure. This is why it is important to guard the minds of our sons in their youth before their choices are negatively influenced.

This points up the irreplaceable role of the father as the guardian of a son's mind, training the son by giving him instructions that develop his mind-set to make good choices towards success. A son who follows his father's instructions will unveil the curtains of success in his life. These instructions become the framework for a son's prosperity. Many influences seek to corrupt our sons' minds to affect their choices, and one of the most influential of these is negative emotions.

In the absence of a father, a son is bombarded by an overflow of negative emotions that affect his self-worth. The fact that he has been abandoned by a father who is supposed to be his guardian in life will cause a fatherless son to harbour negative emotions in his mind.

These negative emotions will attack the mind of a son, causing feelings of abandonment, hurt, and failure, and leading him to blame society for the absence of his father. Moreover, in times of decision-making, the presence of a negative emotion like abandonment can tempt a son into making a decision that puts his life at risk.

The imbalance between knowing the right thing to do and succumbing to these negative emotions becomes the tipping point that drives a son towards wrongdoing. Many fatherless sons, due to feelings of abandonment, have given in to the choice of associating with criminal crowds, even though it was the wrong thing to do. Then, when faced with the consequences of their criminal indulgence, these same emotional influences cause our sons to blame society.

This highlights the critical role of a father and underlines the fact that his absence indirectly affects the choices of a son. With the father present, his positive training and instructions act as a harness that keeps a son in structure, protecting him from the destructive influences of the world that seek to attack his mind and corrupt his ability to make good choices. The presence of a godly father models an example of how a son should wisely deal with obstacles in life.

Within this structure and training, a son can make better choices to become a better son and, consequently, a better father. This is the pattern that mentorships seek to replace by providing instructions to a fatherless son, enabling him to become a father and help break the cycle of fatherlessness. Even when a son matures, he is still subject to these influences because one constant in life is the reality of continuous education. If an individual does not intentionally focus on the positive education they desire, they will still be educated subconsciously by their environment.

I call this negative education influence "sub-education," meaning an education that is substandard to one that adequately prepares a son to be a positive role model and a good citizen of his community. This implies that if a son is not being educated by a positive role model or father figure, he will receive an education from negative influences like his peers, which will shape his mind-set in his youth. This sub-education is dangerous and is a scourge in our communities, especially when it establishes a negative mind-set in a son.

-

PART III

HOW THE FATHERLESS VACUUM AFFECTS OUR SOCIETY

Chapter 7

MISS-EDUCATION
IS TO BLAME

"If I had learned about education, I would not have had time to get into any mischief."

~Cornelius Vanderbilt

As a youngster, I found myself sent away from home, spanning several hundred miles, to attend a Catholic boarding school for boys when I was just thirteen. This institution aimed to cultivate responsibility and impart knowledge in various fields such as faith, business, arts, sciences, and languages. Situated on a vast campus, it accommodated around fifteen hundred boys aged twelve to nineteen. Despite its African location, the school offered a robust British-style education. The staff, predominantly Catholic, maintained strict discipline, led by a headmaster who was a man of the cloth.

However, beneath the education and religious teachings, there lingered a palpable sense of unease within the school's environment. Tales of ghosts and witchcraft circulated among students, set against the backdrop of a community that worshipped ninety-nine lesser gods.

Although there was a structure of discipline established by the staff in authority, the school was essentially governed by the older students, known as dorm prefects, and the elected presidents of the student body on campus. Despite the presence of school staff, it was widely acknowledged that the students held the reins at this boarding school. Bullying, predominantly by older students, was pervasive and manifested in various forms of control. This control was evident through occasional student boycotts of regular class hours, defiance against staff, and sporadic instances of violence directed at certain staff members.

At one juncture, the students, under the leadership of the prefects, orchestrated a mini coup against the headmaster and staff, alleging embezzlement of funds by the school bursar. The housemasters responsible for overseeing the dormitories rarely conducted inspections, fearing the radical senior students, thereby relinquishing control to the students. Rumours even circulated that a bunk bed was deliberately dropped from multiple stories of a housing unit targeting a housemaster perceived as overly strict by the students. The stark contrast between the rebellious actions of young students and the authorities' inability to rein them in left a lasting impression on the impressionable minds of the school's teenage boys. As a young child, I keenly felt the fear instilled by the older students in our school.

Sadly, it was around this time in my school days that my father passed away. Bereft of my father's guidance, I found myself inadvertently absorbing a 'subduction' from the negative influences of my boarding school environment. It instilled in me a substandard, negative education, fostering a disregard for authority exemplified by the rebellion occurring against the school staff.

This disregard for authority during my adolescent years later manifested as a lack of fear for authority due to the 'subduction' I had absorbed. Subconsciously, our school environment had sub ducted some of us into rebellion, and this subduction would echo into our future lives.

EFFECTS OF OUR SOCIETY

The disregard for the law observed in Africa finds a parallel in the form of subduction evident in contemporary American neighbourhoods. When a fatherless son lacks paternal guidance, he becomes susceptible to negative influences prevalent in our communities.

In the book "Dreams from My Father" written by Barack Obama, the author writes that "The absence of a father can have a profound impact on a son's development and well-being in society."

These influences often resemble the harsh lessons taught in the streets, effectively enrolling our sons into a school of hard knocks. In these environments, they learn to disregard the law and engage in constant rebellion against local authorities.

Suppose a young son grows up without a father and his single parent cannot afford to secure him a quality education in a safe setting. In that case, he may find himself drawn to the company of vagabond youth, spending idle time and committing petty crimes. In such circumstances, he unwittingly absorbs a disregard for the law from these groups.

This disregard and absence of respect for the law frequently lead to the perpetration of serious crimes, causing distress among law-abiding citizens in our neighbourhoods.

WHO IS TO BLAME?

Who bears responsibility for the mis-education of our sons? Is it the fathers, whose role is to guide a young boy into manhood? Or is it the mothers, who nurture and shape their sons' development? Should the duty of education solely rest with teachers in our schools, or is it a collective responsibility shared by our communities? After all, as the saying goes, "It takes a village to raise a child." Alternatively, should we fault the governmental structure for failing to provide proper education for our sons?

ROOT CAUSE

If we are to address the issue of miseducation, it is imperative that we address its root cause. This root cause lies in the crucial stages of upbringing at home, when a young man is shaping his identity, and the influences surrounding him lay the groundwork for his mind-set.

During these formative years, the father serves as the first authoritative figure with whom a son interacts. Consequently, the father becomes the gateway to all educational entities, including schools, teachers, governments, and even negative influences such as street gangs. It is the father's responsibility to envision a successful future for his son and to prepare him accordingly. Thus, the true foundation for any positive education for a son lies in the vision and purpose instilled by a father.

EARL WOODS' EXAMPLE

An exemplary instance of a father imparting education through a purpose-driven vision is evident in the case of the late Earl Woods, father of Tiger Woods. Earl Woods discerned his son Tiger's potential during his youth. With a clear vision, he aimed to provide Tiger with an education tailored to his unique purpose, ultimately grooming him into the most outstanding golfer of our era.

Earl Woods's narrative illustrates the transformative influence of a father's visionary guidance in shaping his son's life course. Indeed, I contend that Earl Woods's visionary approach to his son's upbringing significantly contributed to keeping Tiger away from trouble long enough for him to achieve remarkable success in his chosen field. This brings out the notion that when a father instils a sense of purpose in his son's life, the son becomes focused and resilient, capable of overcoming adversities.

Just like in Earl Woods's example, a purpose-driven father can have a vision for his son. When a son lacks a sense of identity and purpose in life, this absence of direction leads to an unfocused state, rendering the son vulnerable to negative influences. Infact, the word speaks of this purpose below:

Spiritual Principle: **'Where there is no vision the people cast of restraint, but happy is 'he' who keeps the law." (NKJV, Proverbs 29:18)**

A PURPOSED EDUCATION

One of the secrets of affluent families lies in the wealth of purpose-driven education they provide. Their success often hinges on the presence of a father figure within the family who possesses the vision to recognize the abilities and inclinations of their sons and daughters. As this father figure identifies the potential in their children, they prepare them to discern their life's purpose through tailored education and grooming.

For instance, if a father is a real estate mogul, he will discern such potential in one of his sons and commence training and nurturing him accordingly. He will provide the necessary education and exposure to ensure his son's success in this field. This approach to education is not exclusive to financially wealthy families. The underlying principle remains the same: even if a father is not affluent, he should still be able to guide and educate his son towards a purposeful life. A prime example is a father imparting the value of service through education, such as teaching, to his son.

This specific training from a father to a son constitutes a purpose-driven education, which perpetuates success across generations due to the visionary guidance of a father. A father must be educated in their own purpose so that they can recognize this potential in their sons and guide them towards success through a purposeful life. Without understanding their own purpose, a father cannot identify the potential in their son and adequately prepare and train him for his own purpose. This education rooted in purpose from a father will enable our sons to navigate past the pitfalls of negative influences that threaten to impact our society adversely.

These are a few key points that apply if you are entering a place of purpose:

- Purpose is typically born from pain.

- Purpose always involves helping others.

- God can initiate a new purpose through you.

- Your purpose has something to do with your father.

- Purpose turns pain into functional passion.

- You can lose your purpose by not fulfilling it.

- Purpose is a source of contentment in life.

- Purpose is not for lazy individuals.

- Purpose connects us with our godliness.

- Serving someone who is fulfilling their purpose will propel you into yours.

LIFE TEACHER

To educate a son in his purpose, a father must possess the passion for fatherhood and the patience to guide his son. These qualities are often present when a father is already operating in his purpose.

Ideally, the father serves as a life teacher to his son, by him being the primary educator on how to navigate life successfully. Achieving this requires significant sacrifice and self-awareness on the father's part. Unfortunately, I've observed that our generations are becoming increasingly self-centred, making it more challenging for fathers to prioritize self-sacrifice in raising our sons.

As the demonstrator, the father teaches through his actions in life, while the adolescent son learns from observing his father's example. For instance, if a father holds a lit cigarette while telling his son not to smoke, the son may still adopt the habit because his father demonstrated it, despite his verbal disapproval. This represents a type of hypocrisy, as a father should embody the positive principles he aims to instil in his son. By setting a good example, the father equips his son with the tools to overcome obstacles he may encounter.

PURPOSE AND PREPARATION

The most valuable education a son can receive is one that instils in him a desire to live a purposeful life, guided towards success by his father's vision. Many individuals have pursued higher education in universities and colleges, only to realize after years of study that they lack passion for their chosen field. Despite their good intentions, they end up investing valuable time in acquiring an education that does not align with their passions or life's purpose.

Instead, individuals should be encouraged to identify their purpose from a young age, fostering a passion for their chosen professions. A son who is guided by his father's vision towards a purpose he is passionate about will save time and money by avoiding the trial-and-error phase, allowing him to gain experience in his purpose at an early age.

Quality education provides the son or daughter with an advantage over many individuals who prioritize a paycheck over their purpose and waste time pursuing the wrong education due to a lack of understanding of their purpose. Therefore, it becomes the father's responsibility to recognize the potential in their sons and commence their preparation and education for their purpose.

Qualty education not only benefits our sons but also helps diminish the cutthroat mentality for survival in our society, as everyone will be operating in a purpose aligned with their passion. This is the true education our sons deserve; a preparation for purpose that is the primary role of a father to his son. The failure to educate our sons to fulfil their purposes is one of the greatest educational shortcomings affecting generations of our sons.

Chapter 8

THE LURE
OF LUST

I beseech you as strangers and pilgrims abstain from fleshly lusts, which war against your soul."

-Saint Peter

There are numerous influences seeking to undermine the upbringing of a fatherless son. One such influence, akin to an assassination attempt on the very essence of a son's life, is the allure of lust—a strong desire for sexual gratification. In the absence of a father, external forces conspire to implant false notions about a son's sexual prowess through self-gratification. This lure of lust incessantly tempts the son, leading him towards developing destructive sexual tendencies fuelled by imagery.

Ideally, when a father is present in his son's life, he assumes the role of a vigilant guardian, shielding his son from the corrupting influences of lust. However, the allure of lust carries deeper implications beyond mere sexual self-gratification. This spirit of lust, which targets fatherless sons, represents a yielding spirit seeking to dominate a son through his sexual desires. It also spawns a controlling spirit that seeks to manipulate our sons through a lust for power and wealth.

In the absence of a father's nurturing and guidance, these yielding spirits seize control over a son's mind, body, and soul, leading him towards self-destruction and detriment to his society.

INCUBUS AND SUCCUBUS

If a son does not submit to the guidance of a father's teachings, he will succumb to other influences. The origin of the word "succumb" can be traced spiritually to a female demon known as "succubus," as depicted in mythological stories where it is said to engage in sexual intercourse with sleeping men. This succubus demon bears resemblance to another mythological figure called "incubus", which is also said to afflict individuals in their sleep. These fabled tales serve as a metaphor that partly enlightens the spiritual attacks faced by our sons.

In the absence of a father figure, these same yielding spirits entice a fatherless son towards negative peers and promiscuity. This lure of lust serves as a destructive force against our sons, and more significantly, it poses a critical threat to our society.

These unclean spirits of lust infiltrate homes lacking a father figure, aiming to spiritually and naturally drain a son. When a father is absent from a son's life, the son may harbour resentment towards his absent father, which can lead to promiscuous behaviour as he seeks validation from his peers. This pattern of promiscuity is exacerbated by the presence of a spirit of lust.

My research shows that this promiscuity differs from a mere lustful spirit; rather, a son's promiscuity is fuelled by lust. This lust serves as the driving force behind promiscuity, greed, and a controlling nature. In the absence of a father, who is meant to serve as a guardian and spiritual guide for his son, unclean spirits like lust seek to establish residence in the minds of our youth.

This is introduced to a son through various means, as these unclean spirits thrive in environments that often exhibit the following factors:

- Lust resides in a home without paternal guidance.

- Lust is prevalent in times of loneliness or idleness.

- Lust thrives in cold and dark environments.

- Lust thrives in the absence of love and compassion.

In the absence of a father's guidance on matters of sexuality, these unclean spirits find a foothold in a son's impressionable mind through exposure to false imagery. One common avenue through which these spirits infiltrate our sons' lives is via the explicit content of pornography readily available on the internet and television. The prevalence of such imagery is heightened in our modern era due to the widespread accessibility of these mediums. Unlike in the past, where such suggestive content was less accessible, today's digital age has made it just a click away.

INTRODUCTION TO DRUGS

This strong desire for lust, stirred by unclean spirits, teaches a fatherless son to be self-centred through the methods of self-gratification. This self-gratification, rooted in greed for money, and a lust for power and control, is exemplified by illicit sexual pleasure. Much like marijuana serves as an entry point to a world of substance abuse, illicit sexual pleasure via masturbation becomes the initial gateway to a lifestyle fuelled by lustful cravings for wealth, power, and control in a fatherless son's life. Combining these sexual influences with the fact that a son has ample free time and a misguided education due to the absence of a father, he is more likely to engage with these unclean spirits through the introductory drug of masturbation.

Commit to a challenge: a challenge for generations of fathers to stand in the spirit of Ezekiel of the bible, as watchmen over our sons' minds, guiding them to safety and instruction, shielding them from the destruction of lust.

SELF-DESTRUCTION

The allure of lust, often symbolized by the spirit of the bull, aims to corrupt a son's mind, leading him into lustful behaviour from an early age. These unclean spirits infiltrate a son's thoughts, driving him to self-destruct by exposing him to HIV and other sexually transmitted diseases that afflict our generations. The biblical narrative of the demon-possessed man in the land of Gadarenes illustrates this grim reality of the enticement of lust, which not only poses a threat to our sons but also undermines the well-being of our communities and states. The narrative reads in the scriptures as follows.

Spiritual Principle: **"For He said to him, 'come out of the man, unclean spirit!' Then He asked him, 'What is your name?' And he answered, saying, 'My name is legion; for we are many.' Also, he begged Him earnestly that He would not send them out of the country." (NJKV, Mark 5:8-10)**

The man, dwelling in the Gadarenes region (Mark 5 verses 1 to 20), was tormented by a lustful, unclean spirit, driving him to reside in dark places, where he cried out and inflicted wounds upon himself with stones. This same spirit, encountered by the prophet Elijah atop Mt. Carmel amidst his confrontation with four hundred and fifty false prophets of Baal, was recognizable by their ritualistic screams and self-harm. Originating from Samaria, where King Ahab constructed an altar to the god Baal to appease his wife Jezebel, who harboured a controlling spirit, this lustful entity plagued the man in Gadarenes.

When the man in the region of Gadarenes, possessed by these unclean spirits, spotted Jesus emerging from the boat, he hurried to meet Him and prostrated in worship. The unclean spirits had driven the man to such a fierce state that Scripture portrays him as untameable, and resistant to any form of authority. Essentially, he was so rebellious that he rejected the control of anyone.

Upon seeing Jesus however, the Bible recounts that he dashed towards Him and bowed in worship, imploring Jesus not to torment him. The irony of his actions—rushing to Jesus and then pleading for mercy—explains the innate human instinct to seek relief from torment, even amidst deep afflictions. But the unclean spirits within him begged for their lives, fearing that Jesus would torment them. This fear stemmed from their recognition of Jesus' authority, as the Father dwelled in Jesus, and Jesus dwelled in the Father.

Therefore, Jesus, possessing authority through his obedience to the Father, commanded the unclean spirits to depart from the man. In a desperate plea, the unclean spirits begged Jesus not to send them out of the region in that country as He ordered them to leave the man.

STRATEGIC ATTACK

The forced removal of our fathers from their homes represents a calculated assault from darkness against the essence of life. Although this displacement may appear incidental to our natural perception, in the realm of the spirit, it is a highly strategic and deliberate attack.

The mention of the name 'Legion,' as the unclean spirits tell it to Jesus, is a tell-tale sign of the fibre of this strategic attack. Legions or armies are highly organized and always possess a strategy to invade. This invasion starts in our homes through the spirit of lust that is introduced to our sons through masturbation, and then spreads like a cancer as this lustful spirit destroys the moral fibre of our communities. As the unclean spirit that possessed the man at Gadarenes was found out, it begged the man of authority in Jesus not to send him out of the region. This is a clear indication that these unclean spirits where on assignment, and sought to continue destroying people in the community, moving from man to household.

This lust that is strategically attacking our sons is not only a desire for sexual pleasure through masturbation; it morphs into even greater lusts within our communities—for money, greed, power, control, and rebellion—ultimately aiming to destroy our society.

HOW DO WE COPE WITH THIS ONSLAUGHT OF LUST?

In an ideal scenario, a son should have a father figure who embodies godly principles and exercises authority over his son. This paternal authority serves as a deterrent against these unclean spirits. Despite the strategic assault on our communities by these entities, the battle against them commences within the home, under the leadership of a godly father.

This is why when these unclean spirits recognized Christ, they called him the Son of the Most High God. Those unclean spirits had seen Christ; therefore, they had seen the Father and were afraid because the Father had all authority. This underscores the fact that God has given natural fathers authority through Christ to overcome unclean spirits in our homes.

However, fathers must walk in the power of their authority through Christ to shield our sons and society. Without a profound understanding of God's presence in their lives, fathers cannot effectively confront the unclean spirits of lust. It is this divine authority that makes these spirits tremble. This authority stems from a father's intimate connection with God, enabling him to act as a vigilant guardian over his sons and society. A father who maintains a close relationship with both God and his son will possess the essential tools of compassion, love, relationship, and the demonstrated power of the Word to defeat these unclean spirits that seek to terrorize our sons and society.

PRACTICE A GOOD PREACH

A father ought to instruct his sons on resisting the allure of harmful images that seek to infiltrate their minds and guide them in evading the clutches of lustful spirits. As a remedy, no unclean spirit can breach the sanctity of the home when a father is vigilant and prayerful over his family. This epitomizes the divine role bestowed upon fatherhood, positioning the father as a watchman, a priest, and a king to govern his household with godly principles. This necessitates not only preaching but also living and teaching by example within a godly marriage to combat these lustful spirits.

As this guidance from a godly father permeates the hearts of our sons, it will catalyse a transformation in our societies, liberating them from the pervasive influence of lustful spirits, with fathers fully embracing their spiritual duty as protectors of our sons and society.

Chapter 9

A CRIMINAL LIFESTYLE

"Nothing better to do, the lure to the youth, the result is usually criminal"

- Ovid

I t is by the decree of God that parents are placed on this earth in the role of parenthood, tasked with offering spiritual and practical guidance to our sons and society. Within this parental calling, which also equips our sons with spiritual and social responsibilities, the father holds the position of authority from which this guidance and responsibility emanate. Without fathers, a son lacks the necessary guidance and instruction to develop the traits essential for contributing positively to society.

When a father is present and lives according to the principles of God, he teaches his son through the example of his own life, enabling the son to become a blessing. In fact, the father often serves as the conduit through which God blesses his son. Without the father's authority over his son, the son misses out on the father's blessing. This absence of a father in a son's life can lead to feelings of anger, as the son misses out on the paternal blessing. In fact, this anger resulting from the absence of a father becomes a spiritual prison that keeps the son's heart in bondage.

This state of being trapped in the heart is perilous for a son, as one who remains spiritually imprisoned and unable to find release may seek to ensnare others as well. Regrettably, many grown men have never escaped the confines of their father's absence and have, in turn, taken it upon themselves to imprison those they encounter. The prison in which our fatherless sons reside is often marked by the cells of anger, the temptations of lust, a segregation unit of promiscuity, and the oppression of negative influences that aim to dismantle a son in the absence of his father.

TRAITS OF ABSENCE

The absence of a father sometimes causes the emergence of certain traits in a fatherless son's life. When a son lacks a paternal figure, one notable consequence is the presence of idle time. To illustrate, we can envision this idle time as a physical or geographical location. If this place referred to as idle time, lacks fatherly guidance, it becomes susceptible to invasion by unclean spirits, such as lust, which seek to take residence in the vacant territory of a son's mind. Since destructive forces are territorial in nature, they aim to establish a stronghold in the heart and mind of a son deprived of paternal leadership. In the absence of a father's guidance, a son exhibits certain traits that serve as indicators of his fatherless condition.

Two traits include:

- A short attention span, where a son is easily distracted from whatever he focuses his mind on and cannot persevere through adversity, reflects the lack of training from his father.

- The desire in a son to constantly seek excitement stems from the absence of witnessing maturity in a responsible father.

It is crucial to pay attention to the traits exhibited by fatherless sons. Remarkably, these behaviours often resemble those seen in individuals involved in criminal activities. This criminal mind-set is not inherent or accidental; rather, it is cultivated during the upbringing of fatherless sons, leading to the development of these traits. This implies that much of the crime observed in our society stems from the spiritual deprivation experienced by fatherless individuals.

HEART OF CRIME

According to Scripture, Esau's father, Isaac, blessed Esau's brother, Jacob. However, Esau did not receive his father's blessing due to his failure to honour him. This angered Esau, prompting him to harbour thoughts of killing his brother Jacob once their father passed away. Hear what Esau said below:

Spiritual Principle: **As Esau hated Jacob because of the blessing with which his father blessed him, and Esau said in his heart, "The days of mourning for my father are at hand, and then I will kill my brother Jacob" Genesis 27:41, NKJV**

When a son is not under the guidance and protection of a father, he unknowingly starts contemplating criminal actions to compensate for the absence of paternal blessing. In Esau's case, he held onto this resentment while pondering criminal deeds until the opportune moment, when he planned to harm his own brother. Despite Esau's father being physically present, the lack of his blessing led him to consider murder as his first criminal act.

How much more, in the absence of a father's blessing, is a seed of criminal thought planted in the minds of fatherless sons? For these sons, whose fathers are physically absent and lack any form of blessing or guidance, the subconscious desire to commit crimes such as taking, robbing, conniving, and stealing from those perceived as blessed in society is deeply rooted.

SPIRITUAL PRISON

This inclination for our sons to contemplate criminal paths originates deeply from the depths of a spiritual prison. Like Esau's contemplation of murder, fatherless sons carry the resentment of not being blessed in society within their hearts daily.

Many harbour the belief that society owes them something, yet it is not society that owes them anything—it is their absentee fathers. Misinterpreting who is responsible for blessing them, they wrongly attribute blame to society or others. This contemplation in the hearts of our sons forms a spiritual and constantly moving prison. The roots of a criminal lifestyle are being nourished by the desire to replace or find the blessing they yearn for, which was meant to be bestowed upon them by their fathers. They will search and exert all efforts to obtain it by any means necessary, even if those means are criminal.

The spiritual prison of anger is just the beginning. Sometimes, their pursuit leads to an untimely death after being trapped in bondage for so long. For the fortunate ones, the journey ends in physical incarceration before death. Spiritual prisons, encompassing anger, lust, crime, greed, corruption, sickness, addiction, and homosexuality, have overwhelmed our society and communities, requiring those who comprehend the depths of these torments and the trials of mental and physical imprisonment to break free.

God is raising a generation from the depths of prisons to liberate those ensnared in spiritual bondage. Many sons, confined to spiritual prisons due to their father's absence, are finding deliverance from God in correctional facilities. Upon their release, they return home or re-join society to aid in freeing others caught in this destructive cycle. Only those who have tasted the bitterness of imprisonment and have been rescued from spiritual bondage possess the wisdom needed to rescue others still held captive by it.

A FALSE MESSAGE

The lifestyle often adopted by fatherless sons becomes another form of mass destruction within our societies, bringing terror into our homes and neighbourhoods. When examining terrorism, the true source of terror can often be traced back to a lack of proper guidance.

One factor contributing to this lifestyle is the misleading messaging of music. These false messages and imagery glorify inappropriate behaviour among our youth, encouraging them to prioritize chasing money, using drugs, disrespecting women, and constantly pursuing worldly possessions. These messages exemplify the traits of the lust of the flesh, the lust of the eyes, and the pride of life. They depict an image of instant gratification, teaching our sons that they can engage in sexual relationships, substance abuse, drinking, and the pursuit of wealth and success, falsely suggesting that this path is not only enjoyable and thrilling but also a shortcut to fame and prosperity.

Without the guidance of a father, a son can easily be led down this path toward a life of destruction and chaos. However, the time has come for a new generation of fathers to be spiritually uplifted, freeing themselves, their sons, and our societies at large from these false messages.

71

PART IV

THE SOLUTION FOR THE FATHERLESS ISSUE

Chapter 10

BREAKING THE CYCLE OF FATHERLESSNESS

"Don't tell me to do something because your father told you. Tell me the truth, and teach me what works"

~ Martin Luther King, Jr.

The issue of fatherlessness is destructive, plaguing our society and serving as the root cause of the destruction not only affecting our society but also impacting our sons and daughters. In the absence of a father, a son becomes vulnerable and is likely to perpetuate the cycle of fatherlessness in his own life and towards his own children. This creates a vicious cycle that continues to erode the moral fabric of our society. Since a father is often the first representation of God's likeness a child encounters, a tainted father figure can lead a son to start life on the wrong path, with a distorted perspective of a father's love and an inaccurate understanding of God's love.

This problem extends beyond American culture; it signifies a spiritual assault on fathers and families, leaving our children vulnerable to early destruction. With universal consequences, fatherlessness becomes a recurring spiritual cycle aimed at undermining the prospects of life, fulfilment, and success.

To dismantle this cycle, we must tackle it at its core. Its origins lie not in a man's fatherhood, but in the heart of a child long before he matures into adulthood.

A SPIRITUAL SOLUTION

Many argue that the solution to breaking the cycle of fatherlessness begins with our fathers. While I agree with this concept, the solution goes beyond surface-level fixes. Fatherlessness and its impact on our sons and society pose a multifaceted threat to physical, emotional, and spiritual well-being, all requiring a comprehensive solution.

The key lies within the relationship between a child and his father. Addressing the root of the cycle begins with society recognizing the profound significance of a son's quest for his father's blessing.

As outlined in earlier chapters, fatherlessness presents major challenges that target our sons during their youth. This onslaught seeks to taint their hearts and minds, severing them from their father's influence. Consequently, as they grow up and assume the role of fathers themselves, they are often destined to perpetuate the cycle of fatherlessness.

Traits such as anger, envy, and lust allure the hearts of our sons, and as they mature, these traits become heavy burdens that drive them to perpetuate the cycle. Breaking the cycle of fatherlessness thus necessitates a spiritual battle waged within the hearts of fathers, children, and humanity as a whole.

This battle must encompass spiritual, mental, physical, and social dimensions, igniting fervour around the issue of fatherlessness that compels fathers and sons to reconcile.

Without a transformation of the hearts of fathers and sons toward each other, the cycle will persist. Despite the inherent wickedness of the human heart and the difficulty in discerning its intentions, a solution must be found.

THREE HEARTS

Both the father and the child bear responsibility in the process of rekindling their bond; while the father plays a crucial role in turning his heart back to his son, the child also holds a share of responsibility in returning to the father.

For the son, forgiving his father for his absence in his life is essential. While it's possible that one's father may not have done much besides being partly responsible for bringing them into this world, extending forgiveness for his absence is crucial. This act of forgiveness not only aids in healing but also initiates the process of reconciliation. While forgiveness is directed towards the father, it is truly a spiritual exercise in healing for the fatherless son.

For the father, accepting responsibility and expressing love for his absence in his son's life is paramount. Assuming this role demands patience, love, humility in approaching the son, and diligence, as the son may perceive it as actions that should have been taken long ago. However, for both the father and son, embodying and accepting these attributes hinges on recognizing God in their hearts. Pursuing this spiritual solution is key to breaking the cycle of fatherlessness in their hearts.

Three hearts must be reconciled in this process: the heart of a father, the heart of a son, and the pursuit of the heart of God. Without sons and fathers seeking the face and heart of God, it will be impossible to break the cycle of fatherlessness in our societies. The attributes of patience, love, humility, forgiveness, and honour required to break this cycle are the very attributes of God's heart. See what the bible says about the healing process that intertwines three hearts.

Spiritual Principle: "And he will turn the hearts of the fathers to the children, and the hearts of the children to their fathers" (NKJV, Malachi 4:6)

This principle regarding turning the hearts of fathers to their children and vice versa originates from the book of Malachi in the scriptures. While the scripture primarily focuses on turning the hearts of fathers to their children, it also encompasses the concept of turning the hearts of the children of Israel to God, their father.

This principle carries significant implications in the spiritual message, relating to both our natural fathers and sons turning their hearts to each other in forgiveness and healing to break the cycle of fatherlessness.

In Blair Linnie's book, "Finding My Father", the author poignantly shares and summarizes through her book, the fact that "The Gospel of God Heals the Pain of Fatherlessness." God is calling his people's hearts back to himself, and as a result, when the hearts of the people turn to God, they will also turn to one another.

THE SPIRIT OF ELIJAH

God sent the prophet Elijah to teach the children of Israel about repentance so that they could prepare their hearts to receive the heart of a God who sought to have a relationship with them.

The prophet Elijah taught many people to turn their hearts back to God. He also rebuked others harshly for the negative traits that tainted their hearts.

Most significantly, Elijah mentored one of the most powerful prophets of his era, Elisha, preparing him as a successor in his lineage.

Several key principles can be gleaned from Elijah's spirit to break this cycle of fatherlessness, such as: teaching the system of God, rebuking a corrupted heart, and mentoring sons into men.

A heart that feels distant from either a son or a father needs guidance to move towards the desired solution. This underscores the significance of teaching, mentorship, discipleship, and relationships as central components of the spiritual remedy for breaking the destructive cycle of fatherlessness.

Ultimately, the absence of an involved father creates a void in the natural relationship one is born into, like the emptiness we feel in our own hearts when lacking a relationship with God.

Like Elijah, fathers in our current generation must adopt the spirit of Elijah, nurturing their sons and imparting godly principles to break the cycle of fatherlessness. Without instilling these principles, our sons will fail to recognize the importance of their roles as fathers in society.

Additionally, lacking a connection with God renders it impossible to empathize with humanity and its challenges. As successive generations turn to God, fathers will inevitably turn their hearts towards their sons.

A SPIRITUAL FATHER

Similar to numerous fatherless sons, I experienced an integral part of childhood without a father, particularly during my formative adolescent years. The absence of a father figure created a significant void in my life, prompting me to seek an identity in unhealthy avenues.

My heart yearned for a father figure to fill this void, hoping to find guidance and love through a nurturing relationship. Lacking my father's presence and guidance left me feeling deprived of his blessing and essential instruction, leading me to wrongly believe I was cursed and compelling me to navigate life with a pervasive sense of inadequacy. This path led me into various troubles, but it was during this time of immense challenges that God provided me with a spiritual father figure in the form of a mentor.

Through our relationship that was centred on Christ, my mentor helped mend the wounds of fatherlessness in my heart. One of the most significant lessons he imparted to me was the principle of humility. This principle was crucial for allowing me to embrace teachings that helped me to forge my identity in Christ through a connection with a surrogate father figure, given the absence of my own father.

This relationship between a spiritual father and son, amidst the challenges of life, resembled what secular society would term mentorship. However, it was a profound mentorship experience within the walls that were grounded in Christ's teachings. It catalysed healing the wounds of a broken man, teaching humility and instilling discipline, all while revealing the blessings found in Christ.

This mentorship not only brought me closer to my own son but also redirected my purpose towards restoring fatherless sons to a relationship with God and the children they had left behind.

A FATHER'S BLESSINGS

Through this spiritual relationship with my mentor, which followed the pattern of father and son, I learned essential traits that truly healed a wounded heart. This relationship taught me how to love and demonstrate obedience. It helped foster greater faith in me and instilled in me a healthy fear.

Through this father-and-son dynamic, I learned to honour my mentor and found myself on a path of purpose. It was through acquiring these attributes that I received and understood a verbal blessing from a father figure, affirming my future success and purpose.

This blessing made me realize that a son who embodies the virtues of love, obedience, faith, fear, and honour will thrive and find purpose in life.

Therefore, when a son practices these principles, it places him under authority long enough to receive such blessings.

If we are to break the cycle of fatherlessness, we need godly men and fathers who exemplify these qualities in their lives and teach our sons these attributes and principles. These men should have received the father's blessing themselves, thereby enabling them to pass on the inheritance of these blessings to the generations of sons to come.

FATHERLESS

Chapter 11

A GOOD MAN

"After seven marriages and losing a lot of money, I realized, I was looking for something I never had or even seen: A good man"

~ Elizabeth Taylor

The absence of a father in his son's life, stretches beyond his childhood. This void in our homes also influences our daughters, shaping them as they transition into roles such as mothers, sisters, rich aunties, wives, entrepreneurs, and working professionals.

In the ten lessons from the book "The Absent Father Effect on Daughters: Father Desire, Father Wounds" by Susan E. Schwartz. The author delves into the profound impact that an absent father can have on a daughter's psychological development and overall life. This underscores the fact that fatherlessness is a global issue. Hence, our societal and structural experiences decline, causing us to miss out on the benefits that a father's presence would bring.

I am referring to the nurturing and guidance provided by a father's love, obedience, and instruction in biblical principles. That equips a child for spiritual and social responsibilities in life. The absence of this guidance results in our children growing up without crucial spiritual and social elements that would enable them to succeed and manage success in society.

Consequently, when fatherless sons and daughters grow up to become parents themselves, they lack the foundational knowledge and keys to effective parenthood, thus perpetuating the vicious cycle repeatedly.

This vicious cycle of fatherlessness makes it difficult for the generations of fatherless children to even recognize what they are missing or what to seek in a father figure. To address the fatherless issue, we must recognize the qualities of a father figure to help make informed decisions in choosing the right man to nurture our sons and daughters.

Without understanding what a father figure entails, the introduction of such a figure into our lives will be delayed, hindering the progress that God has intended for us towards a successful life under authoritative guidance.

A GOOD MAN

A good man embodies God's authority through humanity; a father figure maintains a balance of godliness in both love and authority. This positive authority enables a man to recognize the godly qualities within him, thereby influencing others in a constructive manner through his teachings and his example, ultimately preparing them for success in life.

The godly attribute of love and the balanced authority that God desires for a father is the driving force designed to enable the effective training of a son. Through this attribute, a son perceives God's love reflected in a father's affection for him.

It is crucial for a son to recognize that the man genuinely cares for him and has his best interests at heart. This principle serves as the cornerstone of the relationship between a father and son, a mentor and a son, a teacher or coach, or any male figure in a son's life. It is through the authoritative relationship with a good man that a son can come under the guidance of a father figure to receive life lessons that will usher blessings into his life. In this divine relationship of God, father, and son, pride transforms into humility, and hatred into love. Without this transformation, a son is destined to navigate life unfulfilled.

The trust that is nurtured through the love of a good man will inspire the obedience of a son, which is essential to breaking the cycle of fatherlessness. A good man not only embodies the authority bestowed by God, infused with love, but also demonstrates the patience needed to impart wisdom, knowledge, and understanding to his household as a teacher. Through the obedience of a good man in the life of a fatherless son, God aims to dismantle the grip of fatherlessness in our society, underscoring the importance of identifying such authoritative figures within our communities.

POWER IN AUTHORITY

When a good man aligns himself with the author of the universe, he gains an authority that empowers him to have a significant impact in his home. This does not imply that a good man exerts negative control over a son in need; rather, it signifies that he wields positive influence to guide a son under his discipline, teaching him the fundamental attributes of success that God desires for our children.

This power that a good man possesses stems from his submission to the authority of God through Christ. A good man is entrusted with a measure of power in his authority to overcome the influences of unclean spirits that seek to harm his children's minds. This power was exemplified in Jesus as he healed the demon-possessed boy in the region, as discussed in the previous chapter.

Similarly, God grants His power to a good man, a fatherly figure who submits himself to God's leadership, enabling him to protect their homes and nurture our sons towards a successful and purposeful life. This authority and power bestowed by God upon a man for his household is illustrated in the following spiritual story.

SPIRITUAL PRINCIPLE

A Roman centurion once approached Jesus, requesting him to heal a servant in his household. This centurion comprehended the significance of the authority under which he operated, derived from his willingness to submit to those in positions of higher authority. This centurion received a blessing from God through Jesus to heal his servant in his household. He understood that to possess authority or the healing power that accompanies it, one must know how to submit to authority.

When speaking to Jesus, the centurion said, "For I also am a man placed under authority, having soldiers under me, and I say to one, 'Go,' and he goes, and to another, 'Come,' and he comes, and to my servant, 'Do this,' and he does it." (NKJV, Luke 7:8)

Embodying the role of a good man, the centurion submitted to his own authority, despite being an authority figure himself. His adherence to order and structure under authority mirrored the heavenly order of God, Jesus, and the angels.

This is why he received a miraculous blessing through the power of his obedience over his servant and his household. Similarly, when a good man, such as a father figure, submits to the authority and structure within God's system, he will possess the power within God's authority to bring healing. A good man thus possesses the power to break this cycle of fatherlessness as he is fulfilling his role as a father. For even God in creation saw and said that "it is good" when he saw what he created, because it was performing the function for which it was fashioned.

Chapter 12

MY FATHER
IN HEAVEN

"How to be a father, I know not much, but to lean on God to father me as I was not"

~ OVID

At the age of 15, while attending boarding school in West Africa, I recall sneaking away from campus with some friends to visit another school that was forbidden to us. Unaware of the recent riot involving boys from another school, we were caught by patrol officers upon arrival and subjected to harsh beatings with an assault rifle. Subsequently, we were taken to the authorities, who then passed us on to the student board, where we were instructed to await the arrival of the school headmaster.

As we waited, we were compelled to sit in the centre of the compound. An enraged mob, fuelled by the recent riot and further incensed by our presence, began hurling rocks at us as we knelt. The loose gravel and marble chips struck our bodies, occasionally tearing flesh. I recall bowing my head and praying to God for assistance. Suddenly, we were rescued and swiftly moved away from the furious mob to a safe area where we awaited our school headmaster to begin processing disciplinary action against us for our disobedience.

Whenever I reflect on other instances of deliverance, such as this situation at school, I can always remember the presence of God's hand covering and protecting me. Like a father in heaven, even in my wrongdoing, His protective presence has always been steadfast over me and in the lives of many fatherless sons.

GOD AS A HEAVENLY FATHER

Growing up without my biological father is an unchangeable aspect of my past. I remember facing many challenges because, like many fatherless sons, I sought to find my identity without the guidance of a paternal figure.

In the midst of my father's absence, I have always felt the nurturing presence of a heavenly father in my life. Reflecting on numerous challenging incidents, I recall the vigilant eye of God, which either rescued me from immediate danger or shielded me during times of hardship. This is the same paternal presence that rescues many fatherless sons from near-death experiences. Whether it's being saved from the flash of bullets, a moment of divine deliverance, or being spared from a fatal accident that claimed the lives of others,

God demonstrates His care for the fatherless. For a fatherless son, there is always a heavenly father extending His hand for the acceptance of His children. This heavenly father watches over His offspring, providing in times of need, defending in times of trouble, granting when we ask, protecting in danger, and disciplining in wrongdoing.

His divine intervention is evident in various forms, whether through circumstantial deliverance, assistance from others, the presence of a father figure, or mentor, or even through undeserved favour from strangers. In the absence of a biological father, a son has a heavenly father whom he can turn to through prayer and receive a father's blessing. This blessing is exemplified by traits such as love, obedience, faith, fear, and honour, which are to be instilled in our fatherless sons by God's spirit as a solution to the issue of fatherlessness.

Equipped with these traits, a son will carry blessings wherever he goes. As he grows into fatherhood, he will impart these teachings to the sons of future generations. This instruction in traits may be directly from a heavenly father or supernaturally from God, or indirectly from a father figure who has been granted authority by God to guide future generations.

GOD'S WILL

God's intention for fatherhood is that a biological father serves as a guiding light in his son's life, teaching and leading him towards a life of abundance, success, and purpose. This implies that the presence of our heavenly father is evident in these relationships. When a fatherless son experiences the blessings of such a relationship, he becomes equipped to navigate life on Earth, reflecting his god-like nature.

In the book "Gods Focus on the Fatherless" by Dwight David Croy, the author shares God's repeated exhortations towards fatherhood, brokenness, authority, relationship, presence and justice. Therefore, to address the issue of fatherlessness, we must turn to God. The hearts of both fathers and their estranged children must turn towards God in order for their hearts to be reconciled in relationship with each other.

It is within God's redemptive plan for fatherhood that He sent His only begotten son, 'the Christ', to the earthly realm for redemption. Just as Christ came to reconcile the people of Israel to a proper relationship with God, establish the church, endure the cross, die, and rise again, and release the power of the Holy Spirit, He also came to demonstrate the healing power inherent in the father-son relationship. True Christianity, as taught through the gospel and the master-disciple relationship as seen in Antioch, offered a solution to heal the issue of fatherlessness in my life. This solution is evident in the relationship Christ shared with God as father and son. That solution is evident in the Lords works as we recall his quotes in the scripture below:

Spiritual Principle: **"Jesus answered them, "I told you and you do not believe, the works that I do in my father's name, they bear witness of me." (NKJV, John 10:25)**

The healing power within relationships is available to all nations and their sons. Within the dynamic relationship between God the Father and the example set by Christ as His son on Earth, lie all the attributes that a fatherless son can receive. These attributes include love, obedience, honour, and more, enabling them to exhibit character traits that attract the father's blessing of success and purpose in their lives. It is through this father's blessing that a son or a father seeking to reconcile with their estranged son can initiate the planting of teachings and attributes necessary to break the cycle of fatherlessness.

EARTHLY REPRESENTATIVE

When these attributes can be imparted through the healing relationship exemplified by Christ, God still desires for the nations and their sons to be freed from the burden of fatherlessness.

God has appointed spiritual fathers to fill the void left by absentee fathers, with the aim of teaching the attributes of the father's blessing. This enables the fatherless generations of our sons to receive the father's blessing and break the vicious cycle of fatherlessness.

MY SPIRITUAL FATHER

On my journey as a young man growing up, I always felt a sense of incompleteness in my heart. Despite my love for God and my efforts to live righteously, I knew that something was missing.

While I had a few role models, the absence of my father from an early age meant that I never had the opportunity to witness a live-in example of what a father figure truly looked like—someone who embodied the healing power reminiscent of Christ in fatherhood. What I lacked was the healing power present in the relationship between a father and son, mediated through a spiritual father in Christ.

Then a spiritual father entered my life during one of my greatest trials. God placed a 'man of God' in the role of a father in my life, employing the biblical model of a master and disciple to prepare me in Christ and break the yoke of fatherlessness that had burdened my heart for years.

Having a father figure who has walked a similar path and teaches you during times of hardship holds significant healing power for a son, unlike a distant father figure only reachable in moments of trouble.

God promised to raise someone from among the people to deliver them from bondage. In the state of prison, a man was raised up by God amongst the prisoners, to aid in freeing the prisoners. Similarly, God raises individuals from poverty to uplift the poor and downtrodden.

He is also raising men who have experienced fatherlessness to mentor fatherless sons. Alongside my spiritual father, I learned many principles, and attributes, and lessons of love, obedience, faith, fear, and honour in Christ.

Serving daily alongside my spiritual father, he taught a fatherless son to break free from the pride I had built in my identity due to fatherlessness. With each door I opened and every burden I carried, a bit more of that pride was chipped away. Many questioned why a man would humble himself to serve another mere man; however, it is precisely this lesson—the lesson of humility—that prepares a son to receive the father's blessing.

For it is often easier to demonstrate humility before an unseen God than it is to humble oneself before a seen man in the name of God. Indeed, if a man can humble himself before another man in the presence of others, he likely possesses true humility.

Due to my willingness to embrace humility and receive the teachings of my spiritual father, I was blessed with a pronouncement of the Father's blessing over my life. Love, obedience, faith, fear, and honour became my guiding principles through a period of testing and establishment. Wherever I go and whatever I do, I am assured of success and purpose. These where the pronouncements I received embedded in one of many bible scriptures of which one is shared below.

Spiritual Principle: "**Therefore may God give you of the dew of heaven, of the fatness of the earth, and plenty of grain and wine" (Genesis 27:28 NKJV)**

The above record is one of the notable instances in the bible, where Isaac the Father pronounces a blessing on his son Jacob. Indeed, this pronunciation, after years of relationship between father and son, is the anointing that breaks the yoke of fatherlessness.

Many fatherless sons have never heard a man, or a father pronounce the father's blessing over them, after years of mentorship, and leadership over their lives. The absence of this relationship between a father and son worsens the cycle of fatherlessness.

However, God is raising spiritual fathers from among those who have and have not experienced fatherhood to reverse the tide of this cycle, so they can impart the Father's blessing of success and purpose to our children, so that forever in their generations they can break the yoke of fatherlessness.

AFTERWORD

Can you imagine a generation blessed by their fathers, reaping all the benefits that come with it? Visualize the strength of a family structure where wives stand by their husbands, children look up to their fathers, parents care for their wards, and society benefits from another productive member in the family of humanity.

Amoo has placed fatherhood under the discerning microscope of a heart enlightened by Christ Himself. You can't help but walk away from this book with a deeper understanding of fatherhood. In this book, he gives fathers, sons, nephews, uncles, brothers, employees, businessmen, and church leaders hope to be all that God created them to be.

'Fatherless' can equip us with the tools to break through the darkness and see the light of a new day, enabling the fatherless men of our generation to see again. What Amoo has done in this magnificent work is to help us understand what the prophet Joel said in (Joel 2:28 KJV)

"And it shall come to pass afterward, that I will pour out my spirit upon all flesh; and your sons and your daughters shall prophesy, your old men shall dream dreams, your young men shall see visions:"

I am confident that once you read this book, you will have a complete vision of men fulfilling their dreams of being fathered and becoming the fathers they always wanted to be.

By Bro. Nacoe Brown
Spiritual Father

ENDNOTES

Chapter One

i. New King James Version [NKJV], Revelations 1:18, page 14, the keys to hell and death

ii. Quote accessed December 2011 at http://quotegarden.com

iii. Isaiah 14:12-15, page 25,

iv. Collin's Webster's Dictionary, definition of assassin, page 31

v. NKJV Genesis 3, page 32

vi. NKJV Exodus 1:16 and 22, page 34

vii. NKJV, Matthew 2:13, page 35

viii. Page 36, experimental exercise, story of James Forrest in a conversation with the author on November 18, 2011

Chapter Two

ix. Quote accessed January 2012, http://quotegarden.com

x. Page 47, an experiential exercise in the story of a son as told by Tami Ralston

Chapter Three

xi. Quote accessed January 2012, http://quotegarden.com

xii. Page 50, verbal quotation from spiritual kingdoms teaching by Nacoe Brown

xiii. NKJV, Proverbs 17;11

Chapter Four

xiv. Quote accessed February 2012, http://quotegarden.com

xv. Page 68, fictional name of a true story

Chapter Five

xvi. Quote by Tami Ralston received on email February 2012, page 71

xvii. Page 79, quote by Nacoe Brown in wife material

Chapter Six

xviii. Quote accessed February 2012, http://quotegarden.com

xix. Collin's Webster's Dictionary, definition of choice, page 81

Chapter Seven

xx. Quote accessed March 2012, http://quotegarden.com

xxi. Page 97, a paraphrased story of Earl Woods in relation to a visionary father

xxii. Page 101, quote by Nacoe Brown in wife material

Chapter Eight

xxiii. Quote accessed March 2012, http://quotegarden.com

xxiv. NKJV, 1 Kings 18:28, page 109

xxv. NKJV, 1 Kings 16:32, page 109

Chapter Nine

xxvi. Quote accessed March 2012, http://quotegarden.com

Chapter Ten

xxvii. Quote accessed April 2012, http://quotegarden.com

xxviii. vision of half banjo residence, King of Kings ministries

Chapter Elven

xxix. Quote accessed April 2012, http://quotegarden.com

Chapter Twelve

xxx. Quote accessed May 2012, http://quotegarden.com

xxxi. NKJV Genesis 27:28 page 131

CONTRIBUTORS TO "FATHERLESS"

I would like to express my heartfelt gratitude to the individuals listed below, who entrusted me with the role of guiding them in their spiritual development and provided me with invaluable inspiration for writing this book.

- James Forrest
- Mengasha Clark-Ray
- Eric Maxwell
- Aaron Kee
- James Wright
- Amos Ashcraft
- Marquis Wilcox
- Scott Ridner
- Alexander Majett
- Jamar Campbell
- Jabron Clarke
- Aaron Churchwell
- Lashawn Moncreif
- Kumar Bishop
- Peter Craigg
- Martin Beserra
- Juan Alcocer
- Julio Cesar Cardenas
- Preston Mills
- David Jones

- Thomas Harrison
- Broderick Richardson
- Tracey Redmon
- Elliot Turner
- James Turner
- Tim Shorty
- Cameron Wimzie
- Tyrone Gill
- Jonathan Hunter
- Antwan Franklin
- Tawan Warrick
- Steven Griffin
- Taurean Hayden
- Bryan Planter
- Ricardo Wilkinson
- Jeremy Moore
- Phillip Anderson
- John Feldman
- Jimmel Adams
- Tyran Bascomb

- Kelvin Stephenson
- Joseph Davis
- Leon Talley
- Shannon Aguirre
- Eligio Santamaria
- Alfredo Villalobos
- Andres Contreras
- Jerry McCarter
- Detrick Saulter
- Guy Collins
- Stanley Jenkins
- Kenneth Smith
- Eric Jones
- Reginald McKibbens
- Ronald Jones
- Angel Navarro-Gutierrez
- James Braden
- Troy Allison
- Mike McCoy
- Reggie Fields
- Eugene Jackson
- Donald Williams
- Rodney Wilson
- Jarrode Phillips

- Gumaro Gonzalez
- Flores Garcia
- Alvin Quarles
- Guo Xing-Hai
- Juan Espinosa-Mendez
- Dwayne Jackson
- Chris Walker
- Kevin McCormick
- Terry Herbin
- Juan Garcia-Garay
- Jose Estrada-Acuna
- Edgar Carrion
- Terry Madsen
- Tim Cheatham
- Brandon Hill
- Shaun Shannon
- Pedro Morales
- Eduardo Mejias-Alvarez
- Antonio Espey
- Rev. Jacob Olaitan Olaniyi
- Regina Cyrus
- Ps. David O. Livingstone
- Ps. Alex. O. Boateng
- Danielle Attipoe

About the Author

Nana Kwame Amoo Adare grew up in a fatherless home, experiencing firsthand, the emotional and psychological challenges that often accompany the absence of a father figure. Later in life, he faced the pain of fatherlessness again when his own son grew up without a father present. This cycle led to a period of turmoil where Amoo confronted the deep-seated effects of fatherlessness on his life.

However, through faith and a transformative spiritual journey, he found healing and restoration by discovering a true Father in God. Today, Nana Kwame shares his unique, colourful and rich story to offer hope, healing, and insight to others who may be facing similar struggles. Through his journey, he has come to understand the power of spiritual fatherhood and how the love of God can fill the void left by earthly fathers.

Contact the author directly via kwameamooadare@gmail.com. All rights reserved.

Made in the USA
Columbia, SC
04 June 2025